The ultimate ornament book

Trimming the Christmas tree is a heartwarming tradition that rekindles a childlike wonder in us all. Now, decorating the evergreen can be even more enchanting with our new volume, The Ultimate Ornament Book. *The best collection ever of Yuletide adornments, the book offers more than 140 ornaments to create using a variety of craft and needlework techniques. There are even tree-trimmers that youngsters can make!*

Divided into five captivating sections, the book offers lots of embellishments to help you deck your tree in a way that reflects your individuality and style. Country Charmers features old-fashioned fancies — from barnyard angels to a cone-shaped Santa — all with folksy appeal. Bursting with vibrant colors and fun patterns, the accents in Merry and Bright are cheery delights. For a Nostalgic Noel, fanciful pretties like a beautiful cameo bow capture Victorian romance with a sentimental touch. Elegant Accents has lavish lovelies crafted from rich velvets, golden charms, pearl beads, and more for grand holiday decor. In Just for Fun, you'll find lots of cute decorations and novel designs. A teacher will adore the clever school bell made from a small clay flowerpot, and there are playful tree-trimmers painted with safari animal fur patterns.

Using our step-by-step instructions and full-color photographs, it's easy to create a whole treasury of handmade ornaments — for a lot less money than you'd spend at a department store! This outstanding array of adornments will also inspire you to start a collection to pass on to your children, as well as to share with friends and co-workers. North Pole-tested and pixie-approved, The Ultimate Ornament Book *is guaranteed to deliver spectacular results and a jolly good time to all!*

Anne Childs

LEISURE ARTS, INC.
Little Rock, Arkansas

The ultimate ornament book

EDITORIAL STAFF

Vice President and Editor-in-Chief:
Anne Van Wagner Childs
Executive Director: Sandra Graham Case
Executive Editor: Susan Frantz Wiles
Publications Director: Carla Bentley
Creative Art Director: Gloria Bearden
Production Art Director: Melinda Stout

TECHNICAL
Managing Editor: Kathy Rose Bradley
Technical Editor: Leslie Schick Gorrell
Senior Technical Writer: Kimberly J. Smith
Technical Associates: Margaret F. Cox, Briget Julia
Laskowski, Kristine Anderson Mertes, Alice Crowder,
and Linda Luder

EDITORIAL
Associate Editor: Linda L. Trimble
Senior Editorial Writer: Robyn Sheffield-Edwards
Editorial Associates: Tammi Williamson Bradley,
Terri Leming Davidson, and Darla Burdette Kelsay
Copy Editor: Laura Lee Weland

DESIGN
Design Director: Patricia Wallenfang Sowers
Designers: Sharon Heckel Gillam, Barbara Bryant Scott,
Linda Diehl Tiano, and Rebecca Sunwall Werle

ART
Book/Magazine Art Director: Diane M. Hugo
Senior Production Artist: Michael A. Spigner
Photography Stylists: Connie Bennett Basco, Sondra Daniel,
Karen Smart Hall, Aurora Huston, Laura McCabe,
Christina Tiano Myers, Zaneta Senger, and Alaina Sokora

ADVERTISING AND DIRECT MAIL
Senior Editor: Tena Kelley Vaughn
Copywriters: Steven M. Cooper, Marla Shivers,
and Marjorie Ann Lacy
Assistant Copywriter: Dixie L. Morris
Designer: Rhonda H. Hestir
Art Director: Jeff Curtis
Production Artists: Linda Lovette Smart and
Leslie Loring Krebs
Publishing Systems Administrator: Cindy Lumpkin
Publishing Systems Assistant: Gregory A. Needels

BUSINESS STAFF

Publisher: Bruce Akin
Vice President, Finance: Tom Siebenmorgen
Vice President, Retail Sales: Thomas L. Carlisle
Retail Sales Director: Richard Tignor
Vice President, Retail Marketing: Pam Stebbins
Retail Customer Services Director: Margaret Sweetin
General Merchandise Manager: Russ Barnett

Distribution Director: Ed M. Strackbein
Executive Director of Marketing and Circulation:
Guy A. Crossley
Circulation Manager: Byron L. Taylor
Print Production Manager: Laura Lockhart
Print Production Coordinator: Nancy Reddick Baker

Table of Contents

COUNTRY CHARMERS 6

MERRY & BRIGHT 30

Table of Contents

Table of Contents

COUNTRY CHARMERS

Inspired by our ancestors' frontier spirit and ingenuity, the country charmers in this captivating collection are cleverly made from fabric scraps, fleece, buttons, and other basic supplies. From Santas to samplers, you'll discover a cabinful of Yuletide creations. We begin with folksy tree-trimmings and a matching tree skirt and topper fashioned after Colonial penny rugs. Colorful wool circles and provincial cutout shapes are layered and sewn together using decorative hand stitching. Just turn the pages and you'll find more homespun ornaments to lend an old-fashioned touch to your holiday decor!

PENNY RUG CHARM
PENNY ORNAMENTS, TREE TOPPER, AND TREE SCARF

You will need black and assorted colors of 100% wool fabrics (we used dark yellow, red, burgundy, green, dark green, and tan), black and assorted colors of embroidery floss (we used ecru, dark yellow, red, blue, dark blue, yellow green, blue green, and brown), khaki wool fabric dye (optional; we used Cushing's Perfection Dyes™ Khaki Drab fabric dye), embroidery needle, tracing paper, 3/4" dia. buttons (optional; for ornaments with circle appliqué only), fabric glue, clear nylon thread, and pinking shears.
For tree topper, you will *also* need 5" of floral wire and a hot glue gun and glue sticks.

ORNAMENTS

1. (*Note:* Follow Step 1 to felt fabrics. Felting wool tightens the weave, thickens the fabric, and helps prevent fraying.) Machine wash fabrics in hot water, rinse in cold water, and dry in a hot dryer.
2. To subdue colors of fabrics, follow dye manufacturer's instructions to dye fabrics if desired (we dyed our red and green fabrics).
3. Trace ornament background pattern, page 108, and desired appliqué pattern(s), this page, onto tracing paper; cut out.
4. (*Note:* Follow remaining steps for each ornament.) Use ornament background pattern to cut background from black fabric. Use appliqué pattern(s) to cut appliqué(s) from fabric(s). Center appliqué(s) on background, overlapping as necessary; use small dots of glue to secure, and allow to dry.
5. (*Note:* Refer to *Embroidery* instructions, page 127, and use 3 strands of floss for Steps 5 - 7 unless otherwise

indicated.) Work Blanket Stitch along edges of appliqué(s).
6. For ornament with Christmas tree appliqué, work French Knots for ornaments on tree. For ornament with gingerbread man appliqué, work French Knots for eyes and buttons and Straight Stitches for mouth. For ornament with cat appliqué, work French Knots for eyes and nose; using 2 strands of floss, work Straight Stitches for whiskers. For ornament with circle appliqué, sew button to circle if desired.
7. For second background layer, center appliquéd background on a 3½" square of fabric; use small dots of glue to secure, and allow to dry. Use 4 strands of floss to work Blanket Stitch along edges of black background. Cutting approx. ¼" from black background, use pinking shears to cut ornament from fabric.
8. For hanger, thread needle with 5" of nylon thread and take a stitch through top of ornament. Knot ends of thread together.

TREE TOPPER

1. Trace tree topper background pattern, page 108, onto tracing paper; cut out.
2. Use pattern to cut background from black fabric.
3. For second background layer, center black background on a 7" square of fabric; use small dots of fabric glue to secure, and allow to dry. Use 4 strands of floss to work Blanket Stitch, page 127, along edges of black background. Cutting approx. ¼" from black background, use pinking shears to cut background from fabric.

4. Follow Ornaments instructions to make 1 Penny Ornament without a hanger. Use fabric glue to glue ornament to tree topper background, and allow to dry.
5. For hanger, hot glue center of wire to back of tree topper.

TREE SCARF

Note: Tree scarf measures approx. 15" x 34½".

1. Follow Ornaments instructions to make 26 Penny Ornaments without hangers. Use corner diamond background pattern, page 108, and follow Steps 1 - 3 of Tree Topper instructions to make 4 corner diamonds.
2. Cut a 12" x 31½" piece of black fabric for tree scarf.
3. With 1 diamond shape at each corner and spacing ornaments evenly, center Penny Ornaments and corner diamonds along edges of scarf fabric piece; glue to secure, and allow to dry. Place tree scarf wrong side up. Use 1 strand of black floss to whipstitch edges of scarf fabric piece to backs of ornaments and corner diamonds.
4. For sawtooth borders, trace pattern, page 108, onto tracing paper; cut out. For border on each end of scarf, use pattern to cut shape from fabric. For border on each long edge, draw around pattern 4 times on wrong side of fabric with ends of drawn shapes touching and bottom edges of shapes forming a long, straight line; cut out long border.
5. Arrange borders on scarf; use small dots of glue to secure, and allow to dry. Use 4 strands of floss to work Blanket Stitch, page 127, along edges of borders.

"POTTERY" BALLS

*O*ur pottery-look balls are reminiscent of the old-fashioned crocks used for churning butter and storing staples. To re-create the look of stoneware, we used gesso to texture glass ball ornaments and then painted them. Classic designs and homey torn-fabric bows provide finishing accents.

"POTTERY" BALLS

For each ornament, you will need a 2¹/₂" dia. glass ball ornament; white gesso; light tan, grey, dark blue, and dark brown acrylic paint; stencil brush; small sponge pieces; old toothbrush; small round or liner paintbrush; paper towels; tracing paper; graphite transfer paper; removable tape; and a ³/₄" x 8" torn fabric strip for bow.

1. For pottery texture, use stencil brush and an up-and-down stamping motion to apply 2 coats of gesso to ornament, allowing to dry after each coat.
2. (*Note:* Allow to dry after each paint step.) To sponge paint ornament, dip dampened sponge piece into light tan paint; remove excess on a paper towel. Using a light stamping motion, use sponge piece to paint ornament. Repeat to paint a second coat on ornament.

3. Stamping lightly so light tan paint shows through, use a clean sponge piece and repeat Step 2 to apply 1 coat of grey paint to ornament.
4. (*Note:* Practice spattering technique on paper before applying paint to ornament.) To spatter paint ornament, dip bristle tips of toothbrush in dark brown paint and pull thumb across bristles.

5. Trace desired pattern, page 109, onto tracing paper. Using tape to secure pattern in place, use transfer paper to transfer pattern to ornament.
6. Use small round or liner paintbrush to paint design dark blue.
7. Tie fabric strip into a bow around top of ornament; trim ends.

Coordinating squares of plaid fabrics provide festive frames for our wintry cross-stitched silhouettes. Wrapped in Yuletide charm, the ornaments are trimmed with buttons and grosgrain ribbon. The simple miniature designs and easy no-sew assembly make them quick to finish.

SILHOUETTE ORNAMENTS

For each ornament, you will need a 5" square of white Aida (14 ct), one 3⁵/₈" square and one 5" square of fabric for backing, one 2¹/₂" square and one 3⁷/₈" square of lightweight cardboard, one 2¹/₂" square of low-loft polyester bonded batting, 21" of ³/₈"w grosgrain ribbon, four ¹/₂" dia. buttons, embroidery floss (see color key), and a hot glue gun and glue sticks.

1. (*Note:* Refer to *Cross Stitch* and *Embroidery* instructions, pages 126 and 127, for Step 1.) Using 3 strands of floss for Cross Stitch and 1 strand for Backstitch and French Knots, center and work desired design on Aida square. Trim fabric to 1" from stitched design.
2. Center batting square, then 2¹/₂" cardboard square on wrong side of stitched piece. Fold corners of stitched

piece diagonally to back of cardboard and glue in place. Fold edges of stitched piece to back of cardboard and glue in place.
3. For backing, center 3⁷/₈" cardboard square on wrong side of 5" fabric square. Fold corners of fabric square diagonally to back of cardboard and glue in place. Fold edges of fabric square to back of cardboard and glue in place.
4. Center and glue padded stitched piece to covered side of backing.
5. For ribbon on bottom corners, cut two 3" lengths of ribbon. Glue 1 length diagonally across each bottom corner; fold ends to back and glue to secure. For

top corners and hanger, fold remaining ribbon length in half; knot ribbon 1¹/₂" from fold. Glue each end of ribbon diagonally across 1 top corner of ornament; fold end to back and glue to secure.
6. Glue buttons to corners of ornament.
7. To cover back of ornament, center and glue 3⁵/₈" fabric square to back.

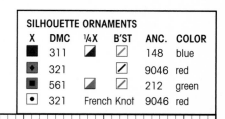

SILHOUETTE ORNAMENTS					
X	DMC	¼X	B'ST	ANC.	COLOR
■	311	◢	╱	148	blue
◆	321		╱	9046	red
■	561	◢	╱	212	green
●	321		French Knot	9046	red

CANDY CANE KRINGLES

You'd never guess that underneath the rough exteriors of these cute Kris Kringles lie hearts of gold — well, actually aluminum foil! Molded into candy cane shapes, the foil is covered with papier-mâché and gesso and then painted. Each Santa sports a uniquely painted hat accented with a tiny jingle bell and a sprig of artificial greenery.

CANDY CANE SANTAS

For each ornament, you will need instant papier-mâché; white gesso; ivory, peach, pink, blue, brown, and black acrylic paint; desired color(s) of acrylic paint for hat; small flat and liner paintbrushes; foam brushes; matte clear acrylic spray; Duncan Snow Accents™ snow texturing medium; small sprig of silk greenery; 6mm gold jingle bell; 5" of floral wire for hanger; hot glue gun and glue sticks; craft knife; aluminum foil; waxed paper; toothpicks; and a soft cloth.

1. Form a 12" square of aluminum foil into an approx. 6" long candy cane shape. Add additional pieces of foil as necessary to fill out shape to approx. 3/4" dia. (candy cane should be firm before papier-mâché is added).

2. (*Note:* Cover work surface with waxed paper. Keep fingers wet when working with papier-mâché. Refer to Diagram for placement of features, using measurements as general guidelines. When applying features, blend edges of shapes into wet papier-mâché on candy cane. Papier-mâché shrinks slightly as it dries, so features may appear too large at first.) Follow manufacturer's instructions to mix papier-mâché. Spread a thin layer of papier-mâché evenly over candy cane. For hat trim, form a 4" long, 1/4" dia. roll of papier-mâché. Apply roll to Santa, flattening roll slightly and joining ends at back. For hat pom-pom, form a 5/8" dia. ball of papier-mâché and apply to end of hat. For mustache, form two 1 3/8" long, 3/8" dia. rolls of papier-mâché; apply to face. Use small pieces of papier-mâché to form nose and eyebrows; apply to face.

3. Use long, straight strokes with craft knife to make texture in beard, hair, mustache, and eyebrows. Use up-and-down strokes with a toothpick to make texture in hat trim and pom-pom. Allow papier-mâché to dry.

4. Use foam brush to apply gesso to Santa; allow to dry.

5. (*Note:* For painting steps, allow to dry after each paint color. Follow Step 5 and use flat paintbrushes to paint basecoats.) Paint beard, hair, mustache, eyebrows, hat trim, and pom-pom ivory. Paint face peach. Paint hat desired color.

6. (*Note:* Follow Step 6 to paint details. Use flat paintbrush for large details, liner paintbrush for small details, wooden end of paintbrush for large dots, and a toothpick for small dots.) For cheeks, mix 1 part pink paint with 1 part water and paint cheeks. Paint large ivory dots for eyes. Paint ivory highlights on cheeks. Paint small blue dots for irises in eyes, small black dots for pupils in irises, and small ivory dots for highlights in eyes. Paint black outlines around eyes. Paint details on hat as desired.

7. To antique Santa, mix 1 part brown paint with 1 part water. Working on 1 area at a time, use foam brush to apply paint mixture to ornament; wipe with soft cloth to remove excess paint.

8. Allowing to dry after each coat, apply 2 coats of acrylic spray to Santa.

9. Glue greenery sprig to hat; glue jingle bell to greenery.

10. Use finger to lightly apply snow texturing medium to hat and greenery; allow to dry.

11. For hanger, bend wire into a loop; glue ends of wire to back of ornament.

DIAGRAM

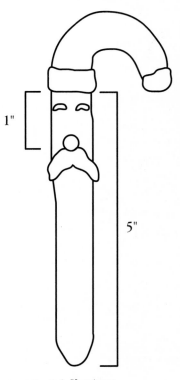

13

CRAZY-QUILT BALL

To create this charming ornament, a large papier-mâché ball is painted to resemble a patchwork crazy quilt with colorful patterns and drawn-on "stitches." The Christmas tree motif is decorated with glued-on buttons. This tree-trimmer will make a great gift for quilters and quilt lovers alike!

CRAZY-QUILT ORNAMENT

You will need a 4" dia. papier-mâché ball ornament, ivory and assorted colors of acrylic paint (we used yellow, dark yellow, red, blue, light green, green, and brown), foam brush, liner and small flat paintbrushes, black permanent felt-tip pen with medium point, tracing paper, graphite transfer paper, assorted buttons, matte clear acrylic spray, and a hot glue gun and glue sticks.

1. (*Note:* Use a glass or cup with an opening slightly smaller than ball to hold ball while working.) Use foam brush to paint ball ivory; allow to dry.
2. For tree(s), trace pattern onto tracing paper; use transfer paper to transfer pattern to ornament as desired.

3. Use a pencil to draw straight lines on ball, dividing ball into several areas around tree(s). Lightly sketch freehand designs on each area of ball (we sketched cherries, stars, and checks on our ball).
4. Allowing to dry after each color, paint designs on ball (in area with star motif,

we used the tip of a paintbrush handle to paint dots).
5. Use black pen to draw lines on ball to resemble stitches.
6. Allowing to dry after each coat, apply 2 coats of acrylic spray to ornament.
7. Glue buttons to tree(s) on ornament.

14

STARRY SANTA

*C*apture the fun of Christmas with our whimsical ornaments! Fabric pieces are fused to a piece of batting to create Santa's merry face. Felt-tip pens and colored pencils are used to shade and add details. For coordinating decorations, assorted wooden stars, like the one accenting the jolly old gent's hat, are covered with homey fabrics.

NO-SEW SANTA ORNAMENT

You will need muslin for face appliqué; fabrics for hat, hat trim, eyebrow, mustache, and beard appliqués; 5" square of low-loft cotton batting; paper-backed fusible web; dark pink, peach, and brown colored pencils; brown and black permanent felt-tip pens with fine points; 9" of jute twine for hanger; tracing paper; small sharp scissors; 1 Star Ornament without hanger; and a hot glue gun and glue sticks.

1. Follow manufacturer's instructions to fuse web to wrong sides of appliqué fabrics. Trace patterns, page 109, onto tracing paper; cut out. Use patterns to cut shapes from fabrics. Remove paper backing from appliqués.
2. Place face appliqué over pattern and use a pencil to trace features onto fabric piece.
3. Make small clips in appliqué between nose and cheeks as indicated by blue lines on pattern.
4. Arrange appliqués at center of batting square, overlapping clipped area of nose over mustache and overlapping remaining shapes as necessary. Fuse in place.
5. Cutting approx. 1/8" outside appliqués, cut Santa from batting.
6. Use dark pink and peach colored pencils to shade cheeks and nose; use brown pencil to shade nose. Use black pen to draw over pencil lines on face and to outline nose. Use brown pen to outline mustache and to draw dashed lines along edges of beard and hat trim to resemble stitches.
7. Glue Star Ornament to Santa.
8. For hanger, knot ends of twine together; glue knot to top back of Santa.

STAR ORNAMENTS

For each star ornament, you will need a wooden star cutout, fabric to cover star, paper-backed fusible web, 6" of jute twine for hanger, and a hot glue gun and glue sticks.

1. Follow manufacturer's instructions to fuse web to wrong side of fabric.
2. Use a pencil to draw around star cutout on paper side of fabric. Cut star from fabric.
3. Remove paper backing and fuse fabric star to star cutout.
4. For hanger, knot ends of twine together; glue knot to top back of star.

NORTH POLE PIXIES

FABRIC ELVES

It'll only take a twinkling for our enchanting elves to capture your heart! You can finish these North Pole pixies in no time at all using nylon stockings and fabric scraps. Sporting cute caps trimmed with jingle bells and holly sprigs, the floppy fellows have magical charm.

For each elf, you will need fabrics for hat, tunic, arms, and legs; an old nylon stocking; thread to match fabrics and stocking; polyester fiberfill; 2 black and 1 red seed bead; embroidery floss for hair; small silk holly sprig with berries; 5/16" dia. jingle bell; lipstick; scrap paper; drawing compass; and a hot glue gun and glue sticks.

1. For head pattern, use compass to draw a 3" dia. circle on scrap paper; cut out circle. Use pattern to cut head from stocking. Baste approx. 1/8" from edge of stocking circle; pull thread to gather circle loosely. Stuff circle with fiberfill to form an approx. 1 3/8" dia. ball. Pull basting thread tightly; knot thread and trim ends (gathered area is back of head).

2. (*Note:* For Step 2, begin and end stitching at back of head.) For nose, stitch a small circle at center of face; pull thread slightly to form nose. Sew black beads to face for eyes and red bead to face for mouth. For cheeks, use fingertip to lightly apply lipstick to face.

3. (*Note:* Use a 1/4" seam allowance for remaining sewing steps.) For legs and arms, cut three 2 1/2" x 8 1/2" fabric strips. Matching right sides and long edges, sew long edges of each strip together, forming 3 tubes. Turn each tube right side out. Knot both ends of 1 tube for arms. Knot 1 end of each remaining tube for legs.

4. For tunic, cut a 3 1/2" x 8" fabric piece. Matching right sides and short edges, sew short edges together, forming a tube. Turn tube right side out. Baste along 1 raw edge of tube (top of tunic). Pull basting thread tightly to gather top of tunic; knot thread and trim ends.

5. For hat, cut a 4" fabric square in half diagonally; discard 1 half. To mark bottom edge of hat on remaining fabric piece, set compass to 4" and position compass as shown in Fig. 1; mark part of a circle on fabric. Trim excess fabric along drawn line. Matching right sides and straight edges, sew straight edges of hat fabric piece together. Clip seam allowance at point and turn right side out. Tack jingle bell to point of hat.

Fig. 1

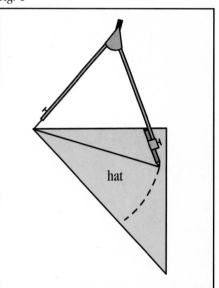

hat

6. For hair, form 5 or 6 small loops from floss. Glue loops to top of head. Glue hat to head with edges of hat framing face. Glue holly sprig to hat.

7. To assemble elf, tack unknotted ends of legs to inside top of tunic. Tack top of tunic to bottom of head. Tack center of arms to back of tunic below gathered neck.

*C*hristmas on Old MacDonald's farm wouldn't be the same without his heavenly herd! These cute trims, made of muslin and batting, are easy to sew on the machine. The bovine angel is covered with painted-on spots. A jute tail and a bell around her neck add to her barnyard appeal. The pig is painted pink and is as pretty as can be, and the gentle lamb's face and legs are also painted on. Each angel is adorned with a wire halo.

BARNYARD ANGELS

For each ornament, you will need two 8" squares of muslin, one 8" square of low-loft polyester bonded batting, ecru thread, black acrylic paint, small paintbrushes, floral wire for halo, wire cutters, gold spray paint, two 2mm black half-beads for eyes, 6" of jute twine for hanger, waxed paper, tracing paper, and a hot glue gun and glue sticks.

For sheep angel, you will *also* need 4¹/₂" of jute twine and a ⁵/₁₆" dia. jingle bell for collar and grey acrylic paint.
For pig angel, you will *also* need 4¹/₂" of cloth-wrapped wire for tail and pink acrylic paint.
For cow angel, you will *also* need 4" of 3-ply jute for tail, 5" of jute twine and a ⁵/₈" dia. bell for collar, and pink acrylic paint.

SHEEP ANGEL

1. Trace sheep angel patterns, page 110, separately onto tracing paper; cut out.
2. With batting square between muslin squares, layer and pin muslin squares together.
3. Leaving at least ¹/₂" between shapes, use a pencil to draw around patterns on top muslin square to make indicated numbers of shapes. Using a short straight stitch and stitching directly on drawn lines, sew layers together.
4. (*Note:* For painting steps, cover work area with waxed paper. Paint both sides of each shape, extending paint approx. ¹/₄" outside sewn lines. Allow to dry after each paint color.) Use grey paint to paint face, lower parts of legs, and ears. Use black paint to paint hooves on legs.
5. Cutting approx. ¹/₈" outside sewn lines, cut out each shape.
6. To assemble sheep, glue legs, ears, and wings to each side of body.
7. Glue half-beads to face for eyes.
8. For collar, thread bell onto twine. Place twine around neck and knot ends together; trim ends of twine close to knot.
9. For halo, spray paint a 3⁵/₈" length of floral wire gold. Form an approx. 1" dia. circle with a ¹/₂" stem from wire. Glue stem of halo to top of head.
10. For hanger, knot ends of twine to form a loop; glue loop to back of ornament.

PIG ANGEL

1. Use pig angel patterns, page 110, and follow Steps 1 - 3 of Sheep Angel instructions.
2. (*Note:* For painting steps, cover work area with waxed paper. Paint both sides of each shape, extending paint approx. ¹/₄" outside sewn lines. Allow to dry after each paint color.) Use pink paint to paint body, legs, and ears. Use black paint to paint hooves on legs.
3. To assemble pig, follow Steps 5 - 7 of Sheep Angel instructions.
4. For tail, paint cloth-wrapped wire length pink. Wrap wire around a pencil to curl; remove from pencil. Glue 1 end of tail to pig.
5. For halo and hanger, follow Steps 9 and 10 of Sheep Angel instructions.

COW ANGEL

1. Use cow angel patterns, page 111, and follow Steps 1 - 3 of Sheep Angel instructions.
2. (*Note:* For painting steps, cover work area with waxed paper. Paint both sides of each shape, extending paint approx. ¹/₄" outside sewn lines. Allow to dry after each paint color.) Use pink paint to paint nose and udder. Use black paint to paint ears, hooves on legs, and irregularly shaped spots on legs and body.
3. To assemble cow, follow Steps 5 - 10 of Sheep Angel instructions, using a 5" wire length for halo and forming wire into an approx. 1³/₈" dia. circle with a ¹/₂" stem.
4. For tail, knot 1 end of 3-ply jute length approx. ¹/₂" from end and fray end. Glue remaining end to cow.

BUTTON FLOWER QUILT BLOCKS

*B*rimming with
glued-on button "blooms,"
flowerpot and basket
appliqués give our quilted
ornaments country charm.
Simple running stitches
embellish the popular motifs,
which are layered with fusible
fleece and homey fabrics.
For quick-and-easy hangers,
jute twine is glued to the tops
of the quaint tree-trimmers.

QUILTED BUTTON SAMPLERS

For each ornament, you will need fabrics
for appliqués, paper-backed fusible web,
assorted buttons, black thread, two 9"
lengths of jute twine, and a hot glue gun
and glue sticks.

For button basket, you will *also* need a
5" fabric square for appliqué background,
a 6$^{1}/_{2}$" fabric square for backing, and a
5" square of fusible fleece.

For flowerpot with buttons, you will
also need a 4" x 5" fabric piece for
appliqué background, a 5$^{1}/_{2}$" x 6$^{1}/_{2}$"
fabric piece for backing, and a 4" x 5"
piece of fusible fleece.

BUTTON BASKET

1. For appliqués, use basket and basket
handle patterns, page 111, and follow
Making Appliqués, page 126. Follow
manufacturer's instructions to fuse web to
wrong side of fabric for heart in basket.
Cut a 1" square from fabric. Remove
paper backing from appliqués.
2. Arrange appliqués at center of
background fabric piece, overlapping

appliqués as necessary and making sure
fabric for heart is centered under heart
cutout in basket; fuse in place.
3. Center fusible fleece on wrong side of
backing fabric; follow manufacturer's
instructions to fuse in place.
4. Place appliquéd fabric piece right side
up on fleece; pin layers together. Press
edges of backing fabric $^{3}/_{8}$" to wrong side;
press $^{3}/_{8}$" to wrong side again, covering
edges of appliquéd fabric piece. Pin
in place.
5. Use 1 strand of black thread to work a
short Running Stitch, page 127, along
inner pressed edges of borders and
approx. $^{1}/_{8}$" outside edges of basket.

6. Glue buttons to ornament as desired.
7. For hanger, knot twine lengths together
approx. $^{1}/_{4}$" from each end. Glue knots to
top corners of ornament.

FLOWERPOT WITH BUTTONS

1. Using flowerpot, flowerpot rim, and leaf
patterns, page 111, follow Steps 1 - 4 of
Button Basket instructions.
2. Use 1 strand of black thread to work a
short Running Stitch, page 127, along
inner pressed edges of borders and
approx. $^{1}/_{8}$" outside edges of flowerpot.
Work long stitches for flower stems.
3. Glue buttons over ends of stems.
4. For hanger, follow Step 7 of Button
Basket instructions.

*A*dd a touch of homespun charm to your Christmas evergreen with these patchwork pretties. Quilt-block designs are stamped onto tagboard, colored with pens, and then bordered with festive fabrics to create the trims. Clipped to a cotton clothesline, the country accents make a merry garland.

QUILT-BLOCK CLOTHESLINE

You will need rubber stamps with quilt-block designs, black ink pad, fabrics for borders and corner blocks, permanent felt-tip pens with fine points to coordinate with fabrics, tagboard (manila folder), miniature spring-type clothespins, cotton cord for clothesline, and paper-backed fusible web.

1. (*Note:* Follow Steps 1 - 5 for each ornament.) Cut a piece of tagboard approx. 2" larger on all sides than quilt-block stamp design. Stamp design onto center of tagboard. Use pens to color design.

2. Use a pencil and ruler to draw a box 1" outside quilt-block design; cut out design along drawn lines.

3. Follow manufacturer's instructions to fuse web to wrong sides of fabrics for borders and corner blocks.

4. For borders, measure 1 side of tagboard square and cut four 1"w strips of fabric the determined measurement. For corner blocks, cut four 1" squares of fabric. Remove paper backing.

5. Using a pressing cloth, fuse border fabric strips along edges of tagboard square, overlapping ends at corners. Fuse corner blocks to corners.

6. For clothesline, cut a length of cord desired length; knot ends. Use clothespins to hang ornaments from cord.

SIMPLE SANTA

The fun shape of our stuffed Santa makes him all the merrier! Accented with an appliquéd face, buttons, and a flannel tree cutout, he has folksy appeal. To accompany the jolly gent, a coordinating garland is made by gluing fabric evergreens, torn-fabric bows, and buttons to a string of twisted paper.

CONE-SHAPED SANTA

You will need fabrics for body, face, beard, mustache, and hat trim; 3/4" x 10" torn fabric strip for bow; two 3" fabric squares and one 3" square of white felt for tree; thread to coordinate with fabrics and buttons; polyester fiberfill; paper-backed fusible web; two 3/8" dia. buttons; an approx. 1 1/2" long twig for tree trunk; 7" of jute twine for hanger; black permanent felt-tip pen with fine point; lightweight cardboard; drawing compass; tracing paper; transparent tape; fabric glue; and a hot glue gun and glue sticks.

1. Use body top and bottom patterns, page 112, and follow *Tracing Patterns*, page 126. Matching dotted lines and aligning arrows, tape patterns together to form a whole pattern.
2. Use body pattern to cut body from fabric.
3. Use face, beard, mustache, and hat trim patterns, page 112, and follow *Making Appliqués*, page 126, to make appliqués from fabrics.
4. Remove paper backing from appliqués. With top edge of hat trim approx. 2 1/2" from top point of body fabric piece and overlapping appliqués as necessary, fuse appliqués to body.
5. Work machine blanket stitch over edges of beard and mustache. Work desired decorative machine stitch over edges of hat trim.
6. Sew buttons to Santa below beard.
7. Matching right sides and side edges, fold Santa in half. Use a 1/4" seam allowance to sew side edges of Santa together. Clip point, press seam allowance open, and turn right side out.
8. Stuff Santa body firmly with fiberfill to approx. 1" from open end.
9. Use compass to draw a 2 3/4" dia. circle on cardboard; cut out. Draw around cardboard circle on fabric. Cut out fabric circle just inside drawn line. Insert cardboard circle into bottom of Santa. At 1/2" intervals, clip fabric extending beyond cardboard to approx. 1/8" from cardboard. Use fabric glue to glue clipped edges to bottom of cardboard; glue fabric circle over cardboard circle. Allow to dry.
10. Use black pen to draw 2 dots for eyes on Santa.
11. Tie torn fabric strip into a bow; trim ends. Hot glue bow to top front of Santa.
12. For hanger, fold twine length in half; hot glue ends to top back of Santa.
13. For tree, follow manufacturer's instructions to fuse web to wrong side of 1 fabric square. Remove paper backing and fuse to 1 side of felt. Use small tree pattern, page 112, and follow *Making Appliqués*, page 126, to make 1 tree appliqué from remaining fabric square. Remove paper backing. Center and fuse tree appliqué to remaining side of felt. Work machine blanket stitch along edges of tree. Trim excess felt and fabric close to appliqué. For trunk, hot glue 1 end of twig to back of tree.

COUNTRY GARLAND

You will need natural twisted paper, two 3" fabric squares and a 3" square of white felt for each tree, paper-backed fusible web, 1 1/2" long twigs for tree trunks, thread to coordinate with fabric, 1 3/4" x 9" torn fabric strips for bows, 3/4" dia. buttons, and a hot glue gun and glue sticks.

1. For each tree, use large tree pattern, page 112, and follow Step 13 of Cone-Shaped Santa instructions.
2. Tie fabric strips into bows around twisted paper approx. 12" apart; trim ends. Spacing evenly, glue 2 buttons and 1 tree to twisted paper between each pair of bows.

EASY COUNTRY ANGEL

EASY COUNTRY ANGEL

Whether adorning a branch or the top of the tree, this angel will make a cheery addition to the evergreen. Fashioned from craft sticks, our country gal is dressed in a sunny apron with a wooden heart "bib." A gold wire halo and a wish-granting wand finish this simple-to-make cutie.

You will need 3 jumbo craft sticks; a 3" square of medium weight cardboard; a 2⅝"w wooden heart cutout; a 1¼"w wooden star cutout; gold, peach, pink, red, and black acrylic paint; medium flat and small liner paintbrushes; fine gold glitter; two 4½" x 13½" torn fabric pieces for dress; a 4" x 6¼" torn fabric piece for sleeves; fabric to cover heart; paper-backed fusible web; tracing paper; graphite transfer paper; two small buttons; two 3" lengths of cotton string; 8" of ⅜"w grosgrain ribbon; craft doll hair; gold craft wire; wire cutters; and a hot glue gun and glue sticks.

1. For head, trace pattern onto tracing paper; cut out. Use pattern to cut shape from cardboard.
2. Paint head and craft sticks peach; allow to dry.
3. For face, use transfer paper to transfer face to head. Paint eyes and eyebrows black, mouth red, and cheeks pink; allow to dry.
4. Use black paint to paint shoes on 2 craft sticks; allow to dry. Glue 1 button to each shoe.
5. Follow manufacturer's instructions to fuse web to wrong side of fabric for heart. Draw around heart cutout on paper side of fabric; cut out heart just inside drawn line. Remove paper backing. Center and fuse fabric heart to heart cutout. Tie ribbon length into a bow; trim ends. Glue bow to heart.

6. For sleeves and arms, center remaining craft stick lengthwise on sleeve fabric piece; spot glue center of craft stick to fabric piece. Fold and glue center of each long raw edge of fabric piece to center of craft stick. Knot 1 length of string around each end of sleeve and craft stick, gathering fabric and leaving approx. ½" of craft stick exposed; trim ends.
7. To assemble angel, gather 1 long edge of one 4½" x 13½" fabric piece between fingers and glue right side of gathered edge to center back of heart. Glue bottom of head to top back of heart. Glue center front of arms to back of heart. Overlap and glue top ends of legs together; glue top ends to center back of arms. Gather 1 long edge of remaining 4½" x 13½" fabric piece between fingers and glue wrong side of gathered edge over top ends of legs.
8. For hair, cut several lengths of doll hair; knot 1 length of hair around remaining lengths to secure. Glue to top of head. Trim to desired length.
9. For halo, cut a 12" length of wire. Leaving a 2" long stem at 1 end of wire, coil remaining wire several times to form an approx. 1½" dia. circle. Glue stem to back of head.
10. For wand, paint star cutout gold; before paint dries, sprinkle with glitter. Allow to dry. Gently shake off excess glitter. Cut a 3½" length of wire; glue star to 1 end. Glue wand to back of 1 hand.

APPLIQUÉS IN REVERSE

Featuring easy reverse appliqués and decorative stitching, our North Woods-inspired tree-trimmers will add rugged appeal to your Yuletide. Moon, star, and tree motifs are cut from fabric squares, which are then fused to solid-color felt so that the shapes stand out against the bright backgrounds. To complete their rustic, outdoorsy look, leather loops with wooden beads are used for the hangers.

REVERSE APPLIQUÉ ORNAMENTS

For each ornament, you will need one 5" square of fabric for appliqué (we used flannel), two 5" squares of felt for background layers, paper-backed fusible web, black tapestry yarn, 2 approx. 1/2" dia. wooden beads, 10" of leather lacing, embroidery needle, hot glue gun and glue sticks, and pinking shears.

1. For appliqué, trace desired pattern, page 113, onto paper side of web. Cutting approx. 1/2" outside outer drawn lines, cut out shape. Fuse web shape to wrong side of appliqué fabric. Cut shape from center of appliqué and discard. Use pinking shears to cut out appliqué along outer lines. Remove paper backing.

2. For first background layer, fuse web to 1 side (wrong side) of 1 felt square. Center and fuse appliqué to right side of square. Use pinking shears to trim felt to approx. 1/4" from appliqué. Remove paper backing.

3. (*Note:* Refer to *Cross Stitch* and *Embroidery* instructions, pages 126 and 127, and use 2 strands of yarn for Step 3.) Work Blanket Stitch along inner edges of appliqué. For star appliqué, work 1 Cross Stitch in each corner of appliqué.

For tree appliqué, work Running Stitch along outer edges of appliqué.

4. For second background layer, center and fuse ornament to remaining felt square. Use pinking shears to trim felt to approx. 1/8" from ornament.

5. For hanger, glue approx. 1" of ends of leather lacing to top back of ornament. Thread beads onto lacing; glue to secure.

PEEK-A-BOO SNOWMAN

*W*hat a sweet surprise this trim will be when hanging from your Christmas tree! Peeking from a mini stocking with a batting cuff, our playful snowman hopes to sneak a glimpse of St. Nick as he makes his rounds. The frosty fellow is a snap to make using poster board, felt, and fusible fleece. His cute twig arms are simply glued on.

PEEK-A-BOO SNOWMAN

You will need one 10" square each of fabric, low-loft cotton batting, and paper-backed fusible web for stocking; one 4" square each of white fusible fleece and white poster board for snowman head; black and orange felt; $^1/8$"w black satin ribbon for eyes; black embroidery floss; 2 approx. $3^1/2$" long twigs for arms; small artificial greenery sprig with berries and a pinecone; a 10" length of raffia; red permanent felt-tip pen with medium point; tracing paper; and a hot glue gun and glue sticks.

1. Trace patterns, page 114, onto tracing paper; cut out.
2. For stocking, follow manufacturer's instructions to fuse web to wrong side of fabric. Remove paper backing and fuse fabric to batting.
3. Use stocking pattern to cut 2 stocking shapes (1 in reverse) from fabric.
4. Matching batting sides, pin stocking shapes together. Beginning and ending $1^1/4$" from top of stocking and using 6 strands of floss, work Running Stitch,

page 127, approx. $^1/8$" inside edges of stocking.
5. For cuff, fold top edges of stocking down $1^1/4$" and glue to secure.
6. For snowman head, follow manufacturer's instructions to fuse white fleece to 1 side (front) of poster board. Draw around snowman head pattern on back of poster board; cut shape from poster board. Place pointed end of head in stocking and glue to secure.
7. Use patterns to cut hat from black felt and nose from orange felt. Use red pen to lightly shade nose. Glue hat and nose to snowman head.

8. For each eye, refer to Fig. 1 to knot ribbon; trim ribbon ends close to knot. Glue knot to face.

Fig. 1

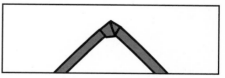

9. For each arm, insert 1 end of 1 twig between layers at 1 side of stocking; glue to secure.
10. Glue greenery sprig to stocking front.
11. For hanger, knot ends of raffia together; glue knot to back of cuff.

CRAFT STICK CHARACTERS

MINI FENCE-POST PALS

Jumbo craft sticks let you create teeny versions of the popular fence-post characters. These merry minis are so inexpensive to craft, you'll want to make some to give as gifts, too! The snowman is cleverly embellished with twig arms, a raffia bow tie, and a paper hat. His smiling face is simply painted on. For our darling angel, we added twisted paper wings, raffia hair, a grapevine halo, and a torn-fabric bow to a painted craft stick accented with star stickers.

For each ornament, you will need a jumbo craft stick, white acrylic paint, flat paintbrush, 5" of floral wire for hanger, and a hot glue gun and glue sticks.

For snowman, you will *also* need orange and black dimensional paint, brown acrylic paint, stencil brush, tracing paper, soft cloth, black poster board, green raffia, a small silk flower, and two approx. 3" long twigs for arms.

For angel, you will *also* need peach, pink, dark pink, and black acrylic paint; white and gold glitter paint; small paintbrushes; natural twisted paper; natural raffia; 1/2"w gold self-adhesive stars; 1/2" x 10" torn fabric strip for bow; and a 7 1/2" length of grapevine for halo.

SNOWMAN

1. (*Note:* Allow to dry after each paint step.) Paint craft stick white. To add texture, use stencil brush and an up-and-down stamping motion to apply another coat of white paint to stick.

2. To antique stick, mix 1 part brown paint with 1 part water. Apply paint mixture to stick; quickly remove excess with soft cloth.

3. For hat, trace pattern onto tracing paper; cut out. Use pattern to cut hat from black poster board. Glue hat to 1 end (top) of craft stick. Glue flower to hat.

4. Paint 2 black dots for eyes and several smaller black dots for mouth. Paint orange carrot shape for nose.

5. For arms, glue 1 end of each twig to back of stick.

6. Tie several strands of raffia together into a bow around neck of snowman; trim ends.

7. For hanger, bend wire into a loop; glue ends to back of ornament.

ANGEL

1. (*Note:* Allow to dry after each paint step.) Paint craft stick white. For face, paint approx. 1" at 1 end (top) of stick peach. Paint black eyes, dark pink mouth, and pink cheeks on face.

2. Apply stars to body. Outline stars with white glitter paint. Paint gold glitter dots on body.

3. Tie fabric strip into a bow around neck; trim ends.

4. For hair, cut several lengths of raffia; knot 1 length of raffia around remaining lengths to secure. Glue to top of head. Trim as desired.

5. For wings, cut a 5" length of twisted paper. Untwist paper, then twist paper once at center to form wings. Glue wings to back of angel.

6. For halo, coil vine into an approx. 1" dia. circle; glue halo to head. Apply stars to halo.

7. For hanger, bend wire into a loop; glue ends to back of ornament.

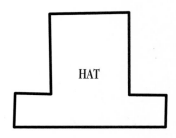

HAT

MERRY & BRIGHT

Capturing the magic that makes us feel like kids again, this fun assortment of Yuletide trims features endearing characters and whimsical charmers! You'll discover enchanting holiday decorations like cheery miniature painted birdhouses, a tiny teddy all abloom, and colorful muslin stars beaming with good cheer! Shown here are two large stars painted to resemble crazy quilts and several smaller ones decorated with single patterns. There are even projects in this collection especially for youngsters. With a little help, kids can make our Christmas tree frame, festive felt stockings, cute paper plate Santa, and more. Designed to tickle your fancy, our jovial jollies are created using a host of crafting materials and techniques — and most can be made in a jiffy!

BRIGHT STARS

BRIGHT AND SHINY STARS

For each star, you will need muslin, white gesso, assorted colors of acrylic paint, small round and flat paintbrushes, fine sandpaper, tack cloth, glossy clear acrylic spray, 7" of 1/8"w satin ribbon for hanger, tracing paper, and a hot glue gun and glue sticks.

For small star, you will *also* need poster board, low-loft polyester bonded batting, and craft glue.

For large star, you will *also* need polyester fiberfill, fabric marking pencil, and ecru thread.

SMALL STAR

1. Trace small star pattern onto tracing paper; cut out.
2. Use pattern to cut 1 star each from poster board and batting. Leaving at least 1/2" between shapes, use a pencil to draw around pattern twice on muslin. For ornament front, cut out 1 muslin star 1/2" outside drawn lines. For ornament back, cut out remaining star along drawn lines.

3. Use craft glue to glue batting star to poster board star.
4. At 1/2" intervals, clip edges of larger muslin star to 1/16" from drawn lines.
5. Center poster board star batting side down on large muslin star. Alternating sides and pulling muslin taut, use craft glue to glue clipped edges of muslin to back of poster board star; glue small muslin star to back of padded star. Allow to dry.
6. Apply gesso to star and allow to dry; lightly sand star and wipe with tack cloth to remove dust. Repeat.
7. Paint star with basecoat color; allow to dry.
8. Use a pencil (and ruler if desired) to lightly draw desired designs on star.
9. Allowing to dry after each color, paint designs on star (we used the tip of a paintbrush handle to paint dots).

10. Allowing to dry after each coat, apply 2 coats of acrylic spray to star.
11. For hanger, fold ribbon length in half; hot glue ends to back of star.

LARGE STAR

1. Trace large star pattern onto tracing paper; cut out.
2. Use pattern and follow *Sewing Shapes*, page 126, to make star from two 7" squares of muslin. Firmly stuff star with fiberfill and sew final closure by hand.
3. Follow Step 6 of Small Star instructions.
4. Use a pencil (and ruler if desired) to divide star into several sections.
5. Follow Steps 7 - 9 of Small Star instructions to paint each section of star. Paint lines to resemble stitches along edges of each section; allow to dry.
6. Follow Steps 10 and 11 of Small Star instructions.

NAMELY STOCKINGS

*I*t's a snap to make these
festive stocking ornaments!
Children can glue the felt
pieces together and help
you add the "stitching"
and names with white
dimensional paint. Fun
and easy, these trimmers
will encourage the whole
family to get involved in
decorating for the holidays.

FELT STOCKINGS

Note: These ornaments were designed to
be fun and easy for children to make. For
young children, you may want to cut out
and paint the felt shapes so the ornaments
will be ready to assemble.

For each stocking, you will need assorted
colors of felt, 7" of ⅝"w ribbon for
hanger, white dimensional paint in
squeeze bottle with fine tip, tracing paper,
and craft glue.

1. Trace stocking, cuff, toe, and desired
appliqué pattern(s), page 115, onto
tracing paper; cut out. Use patterns to
cut 2 stocking shapes and 1 of each
remaining shape from felt.
2. Use paint to personalize cuff and paint
dashed lines to resemble stitches along
edges of cuff, toe, and desired
appliqué(s); allow to dry.

3. Apply a thin line of glue along side and
bottom edges of 1 stocking shape. Place
remaining stocking shape over first
stocking shape and press glued edges
together. With top of cuff extending

approx. ½" above top of stocking, center
and glue cuff to stocking. Glue toe and
appliqué(s) to stocking. Allow to dry.
4. For hanger, fold ribbon length in half
and glue ends to back of cuff; allow to dry.

POINSETTIA BEAR

*A*ll abloom, our
tiny teddy is adorned
with a muffler of velvety
poinsettia petals. A
coordinating gingham
bow embellishes his collar,
too. Sitting among the
tree branches, he'll make
a "beary" cute trim!

POINSETTIA BEAR

You will need a 4"h jointed teddy bear, an
approx. 5" dia. velvet poinsettia, silk
leaves, 7" of ³/₈"w ribbon, cosmetic blush,
and a hot glue gun and glue sticks.

1. Remove petals from poinsettia.
2. Trimming stems as necessary, glue
petals and leaves around bear's head.
3. Tie ribbon into a bow; trim ends. Glue
bow to bear.
4. Use fingertip to apply blush to
bear's cheeks.

SUPER-EASY SNOWBALLS

*P*lain glass balls are
easily transformed into
wintry wonders with a few
simple additions. Crafting
foam is used for the
snowman's mouth and hat,
and his nose is a piece
of twisted paper. A scrap-
flannel scarf is glued on. The
snowball ornament is super
quick to finish, too! The
words are written on with a
felt-tip pen, and artificial
snow is glued to the ball.

CHEERFUL SNOWBALLS

For each ornament, you will need a white
2³/₄" dia. glass ball ornament and a black
permanent felt-tip pen with medium point.
For snowman ornament, you will *also*
need ¹/₁₆" thick black crafting foam,
1" of orange twisted paper for nose, a
1¹/₄" x 5" fabric strip for scarf, black
acrylic paint, small paintbrush, a drawing
compass, and a hot glue gun and
glue sticks.
For "Let it snow!" ornament, you will
also need craft glue and artificial snow.

SNOWMAN ORNAMENT

1. For hat, use compass to draw a
1⁵/₈" dia. circle on foam; cut out. Cut a
smaller circle at center of foam circle to
form a ring that will fit around cap of
ornament. Place ring at base of ornament
cap and glue in place. Paint ornament
cap black; allow to dry.
2. For nose, trim 1 end of twisted paper at
an angle to form a point. Glue large end of
nose to ornament.

3. For mouth, cut six approx. ¹/₄"w
irregular shapes from foam. Glue shapes
to ornament.
4. Use black pen to draw eyes on
ornament.
5. For scarf, make ³/₄" clips at approx. ¹/₈"
intervals in each end of fabric strip for
fringe. Loosely knot fabric strip at center.
Glue knot to bottom of ornament.

"LET IT SNOW!" ORNAMENT

1. Use black pen to write "Let it snow!" on
ornament.
2. Spread glue over approx. half of
ornament and sprinkle with artificial
snow; allow to dry.

Sporting baby sock caps and plaid fabric bow ties, these Yuletide friends are crafted by machine sewing layers of wool or fusible fleece. Their happy-go-lucky faces and other features are painted on. These characters are sure to delight one and all!

You will need fabric for tie, a baby sock for hat, a $3/4$" dia. pom-pom, clear nylon thread, pink and black acrylic paint, small paintbrushes, pencil with unused eraser, disappearing ink fabric marking pen, tracing paper, liquid fray preventative, and a hot glue gun and glue sticks.

For snow boy ornament, you will *also* need two 6" squares of fusible fleece and orange acrylic paint.

For gingerbread boy ornament, you will *also* need two 6" squares of tan wool fabric; a 6" square of white fleece; paper-backed fusible web; white, blue, and brown acrylic paint; and a black permanent felt-tip pen with fine point.

SNOW BOY

1. Trace snow boy and bow tie patterns, page 116, onto tracing paper; cut out.
2. Follow manufacturer's instructions to fuse fleece squares together with fusible sides facing.
3. (*Note:* Use nylon thread for all sewing steps.) Use fabric marking pen to draw around snow boy pattern at center of fleece. Using a short stitch length, sew directly on pen lines. Cutting approx. $1/8$" outside stitching lines, cut out snow boy.
4. Paint orange carrot shape for nose. Use tip of paintbrush handle to paint black dots for eyes, mouth, and buttons. Use unused pencil eraser to paint pink dots for cheeks. Allow to dry.
5. For hat, turn sock wrong side out; cut $2^1/2$" of ribbing from sock. Baste $1/4$" from raw edge of ribbing. Pull basting thread,

drawing up gathers tightly; knot thread and trim ends. Turn ribbing right side out. Tack pom-pom to top of hat. Fold bottom of hat approx. $1/4$" to right side for cuff. Glue hat to head.
6. Use bow tie pattern to cut tie from fabric. Apply fray preventative to edges of tie. Glue tie to snow boy.
7. For hanger, thread a 6" length of nylon thread through back of hat; knot and trim ends.

GINGERBREAD BOY

1. Trace gingerbread boy, bow tie, and vest patterns, page 116, onto tracing paper; cut out.
2. Follow manufacturer's instructions to fuse web to wrong sides of fabric squares. Remove paper backing. Fuse 1 fabric square to each side of fleece.
3. Follow Step 3 of Snow Boy instructions to make gingerbread boy from fused fabric.
4. (*Note:* Allow to dry after each paint color.) Use fabric marking pen to draw around vest pattern on gingerbread boy. Paint vest blue. Use tip of paintbrush handle to paint black dots for eyes. Use unused pencil eraser to paint pink dots for cheeks. Use brown paint to paint over stitching line. Paint white trim on arms and legs and use tip of paintbrush handle to paint white dots for buttons on vest. Use black pen to draw mouth.
5. Follow Steps 5 - 7 of Snow Boy instructions for hat, tie, and hanger.

MERRY MINI BIRDHOUSES

*Y*ou don't have to be a bird lover to appreciate these colorful minis! Painted in vibrant hues and fun patterns, our small birdhouse ornaments will make charming trims for the evergreen. Because they're finished in no time at all, you can make plenty for decorating the tree, as well as all through the house.

CHEERY BIRDHOUSES

For each birdhouse, you will need a 2⁷/₈"h wooden birdhouse, desired colors of acrylic paint, small round and flat paintbrushes, fine sandpaper, tack cloth, 8" of jute twine, and a hot glue gun and glue sticks.

1. Lightly sand birdhouse; wipe with tack cloth to remove dust.
2. Allowing to dry after each paint color, paint birdhouse as desired (we used the tip of a paintbrush handle to paint dots).
3. For hanger, knot ends of twine together; trim ends close to knot. Glue knot to top of house.

PAPER PLATE SANTA

*hildren will have
lots of fun crafting our easy
paper plate Santa with his
red pom-pom nose — he
can be made in a flash! His
festive hat is trimmed with
a white pom-pom and a silk
holly sprig. Iridescent glitter
provides a twinkling finish.*

PAPER PLATE SANTA

Note: This ornament was designed to be
fun and easy for children to make. For
young children, you may want to cut out
the pieces so the ornament will be ready
to paint and assemble.

You will need a 9" dia. paper plate, peach
and red acrylic paint, foam brushes,
iridescent glitter, one 3/4" dia. red and one
1" dia. white pom-pom, silk holly leaves,
black felt-tip pen, spring-type clothespins,
tracing paper, and craft glue.

1. Cut head and hat pieces from plate
(Fig. 1). For mustache, trace pattern onto
tracing paper; cut out. Use pattern to cut
mustache from remaining piece of plate.

Fig. 1

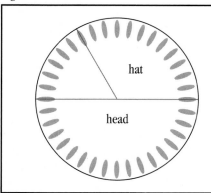

2. Painting on bottom (right side) of each
piece, use foam brush to paint all but rim
of head piece peach and all but rim of hat
piece red; allow to dry.
3. For head, roll head piece into a cone
shape, overlapping straight edges approx.
1". Glue edges together, using a clothespin
to hold edges together until glue is dry.
Repeat to make hat from hat piece.
4. Aligning overlapped edges of head and
hat (back of Santa), glue hat to head and

bend top of hat to 1 side. Glue mustache
to Santa. Allow to dry.
5. Use a clean foam brush to apply a thin
layer of glue to mustache and rim of hat.
Sprinkle glitter on glue, allow to dry, and
shake off excess glitter.
6. Glue pom-poms and holly leaves to
Santa; allow to dry.
7. Use black pen to draw dots for eyes
on face.

REINDEER CANDY CANES

Transform plain candy canes into rascally reindeer with our clever cover-ups. Sewn from felt, the enchanting fellows are rounded up with ribbon bridles, chenille-stem antlers, wiggle eyes, and red pom-pom noses. Whether used as tree-trimmers or party favors, they'll be a real treat at Christmas!

CANDY CANE REINDEER

For each reindeer, you will need a 5³/₄"h candy cane, two 4" squares of tan felt, a 2" square of cream felt, thread to match tan felt, brown chenille stem, two 7mm x 10mm wiggle eyes, a ³/₈" dia. red pom-pom, 2¹/₂" of ¹/₈"w ribbon for bridle, 6" of ¹/₈"w ribbon for bow, 7" of ¹/₈"w ribbon for hanger, two gold sequin stars, removable fabric marking pen, toothpick (if needed), tracing paper, and a hot glue gun and glue sticks.

1. Trace patterns, page 116, onto tracing paper; cut out.
2. Place tan felt squares together. Use fabric marking pen to draw around head pattern at center of felt squares. Using a short stitch length and leaving bottom edge open, stitch along drawn lines. Cutting approx. ¹/₈" outside stitching line and along drawn line at bottom, cut out reindeer head.
3. For ears, use patterns to cut 2 ears from remaining tan felt and 2 inner ears from cream felt. Center and glue inner ear pieces to ear pieces.
4. To attach each ear to head, cut a ¹/₄" long slit on 1 side of head approx. ³/₄"

from top. Pinching bottom of ear to gather, insert bottom of ear into slit. If necessary, use toothpick to help push ear into slit. Glue to secure.
5. For bridle, glue 2¹/₂" ribbon length around nose. Glue 1 star sequin to each side of bridle.
6. Glue eyes and pom-pom to head.
7. For antlers, cut one 2¹/₂" length and two 1³/₄" lengths from chenille stem. Bend

2¹/₂" length in half to form "V" shape. Twist one 1³/₄" length around each end of 2¹/₂" length; arrange to resemble antlers. Glue antlers to top of head.
8. For hanger, fold 7" ribbon length in half and glue ends to top of head.
9. Carefully insert candy cane into reindeer head; tie 6" ribbon length into a bow around reindeer neck and trim ends.

CHRISTMAS TREE FRAME

What a delightful gift this festive frame will make for a parent or grandparent. And it's so easy, children can help make it! A tree shape cut from crafting foam is topped with a yellow foam star and sprinkled with a confetti of polka dot "ornaments" to create the frame. The round opening in the center is perfect for displaying a favorite photo. A ribbon bow glued at the bottom adds the finishing touch.

CHRISTMAS TREE FRAME

Note: This ornament was designed to be fun and easy for children to make. For young children, you may want to cut out the foam shapes so the ornament will be ready to assemble.

You will need photo to fit a 2¼" dia. opening; yellow, green, and assorted colors of ¹⁄₁₆" thick crafting foam; 2"w purchased bow; 5" of ⅛"w satin ribbon for hanger; tracing paper; ¼" hole punch; and a low-temperature hot glue gun and glue sticks.

1. Trace patterns, page 117, onto tracing paper; cut out. Use patterns to cut frame front and frame back from green foam and star from yellow foam. Use photograph pattern to cut desired area from photograph.

2. For ornaments on tree, use hole punch to punch circles from desired colors of foam.

3. Glue star, ornaments, and bow to frame front.

4. Glue photo at center of frame back. Centering photo in opening in frame front, glue edges of frame back to back of frame front.

5. For hanger, fold ribbon in half; glue ends to top back of ornament.

FANCIFUL SANTA

MERRY BEAD SANTA

For a merry St. Nick who's a little out of the ordinary, try our fanciful fellow. His hat, face, and body are made from a modeling compound, and festive beads are strung together for his arms and legs. To coordinate, a garland is made by stringing matching beads onto a strip of checked fabric.

You will need white, peach, and red polymer clay; glossy clear acrylic spray; two black 3mm glass beads for eyes; assorted wooden and pewter beads; clear nylon thread; needle; craft knife; cutting mat or thick layer of newspaper; tracing paper; waxed paper; rolling pin; a toothpick; and a hot glue gun and glue sticks.

1. Trace patterns, page 118, onto tracing paper; cut out.
2. Place cutting mat on work surface; cover cutting mat with waxed paper. Follow manufacturer's instructions to mix small amounts of red and white clay together to make pink clay for cheeks and mouth. Use rolling pin to roll out pink clay to approx. 1/16" thickness and white and red clay to approx. 1/8" thickness.
3. Use a pencil to draw around patterns on clay to make 2 cheeks and 1 of each remaining shape. Use craft knife to cut out pieces. Use toothpick to make holes in body piece as indicated by dots on pattern. Form an approx. 1/4" dia. 1/2" long roll of peach clay for nose and an approx. 1/16" dia. ball of pink clay for mouth.
4. Overlapping pieces as necessary, press pieces together to form Santa head and body. Press 3mm beads into face for eyes.
5. Follow manufacturer's instructions to harden clay.
6. Spray Santa with acrylic spray; allow to dry.
7. For each arm and leg, fold a 12" length of thread in half and loop through hole in body (Fig. 1). Thread ends of thread onto needle and thread wooden and pewter beads onto thread until arm or leg is desired length (we used 7 beads for each arm and leg). For last bead, thread only 1 end of thread through bead, then knot ends of thread together at bottom of bead

and trim ends (Fig. 2). Place a dot of glue on knot to secure.

Fig. 1

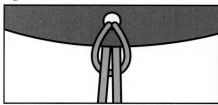

Fig. 2

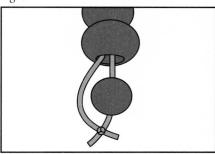

8. Glue beads to Santa for buttons and pom-pom on hat.
9. For hanger, knot ends of an 8" length of thread together; trim ends. Glue knot to back of hat.

BEADED GARLAND

For each length of garland, you will need a 1 1/2"w fabric strip desired length of garland, large needle, assorted wooden and pewter beads, and a hot glue gun and glue sticks.

1. Fold long edges of fabric strip approx. 1/2" to wrong side; spot glue to secure. Thread fabric strip onto needle and knot 1 end.
2. Thread beads onto fabric strip in groups of 3, spacing groups approx. 3" apart. Glue beads to fabric strip to secure if necessary. Remove needle and knot remaining end of fabric strip.

POP-TOP ANGELS

These clever cuties are fashioned from flattened single-serving juice cans. Painted white and sprinkled with glitter, the cans become whimsical angels with painted-on faces, curly hair, and starry halos. Sheer white wired-ribbon bows are glued to their backs for wings.

RECYCLED CAN ANGELS

For each angel, you will need a 5.5-ounce aluminum beverage can; white spray paint; white, peach, red, and black acrylic paint; small round paintbrushes; 5/16" dia. wooden peg for nose; curly doll hair; 6 1/2" of gold wired star garland; 26" of 1 1/2"w iridescent white wired ribbon; iridescent glitter; craft glue; and a hot glue gun and glue sticks.

1. Remove pull tab from top of can. Flatten can with top of can (face of angel) at top. For nose, hot glue peg just above can opening.
2. (*Note:* Allow to dry after each paint color.) Spray paint can white. For face, paint top of can and peg peach. For mouth, paint inside of can opening red. Paint black dots for eyes. Use tip of paintbrush handle to paint white highlights in eyes. Paint cheeks with a mixture of 1 part red paint and 1 part water.
3. To apply glitter, mix 1 part craft glue with 1 part water. Brush diluted glue on body of angel and sprinkle with glitter; allow to dry. Shake off excess glitter.
4. Hot glue hair around face of angel.
5. For halo, form star garland into an approx. 2 1/2" dia. circle; hot glue to head of angel.
6. Tie ribbon into an approx. 6 1/2"w bow; trim ends. Hot glue bow to center back of angel.

CLOTHESPIN SNOWMEN

These jaunty fellows are such a friendly sight! To make the cute characters, we painted large, old-fashioned clothespins and topped them off with wooden spool hats. The ends of toothpicks make clever little noses, and chenille stems form their arms. With their smiling faces and merry accents, these snowmen are sure to find a warm place in your heart!

CLOTHESPIN SNOWMEN

For each snowman, you will need a 5⅞"h wooden craft clothespin; a 1"h wooden spool and a 1¼" dia. wooden circle cutout for hat; two ¾"w wooden star cutouts; one ¾"w wooden heart cutout; round toothpick for nose; 6½" of black chenille stem for arms; 5½" of ⅜"w ribbon for scarf; 2½" of ⅜"w ribbon for hatband; 8" of ⅛"w ribbon for hanger; white, orange, red, green, and black acrylic paint; small paintbrushes; small nail; hammer; and a low-temperature hot glue gun and glue sticks.

1. (*Note:* Allow to dry after each paint step.) Paint clothespin white, spool and circle cutout black, star cutouts green, and heart cutout red.

2. For nose, paint half of toothpick orange; cut a ½" piece from orange end of toothpick. Use hammer and nail to make a small hole in clothespin. Glue large end of nose into hole.

3. Paint black eyes, mouth, and buttons on snowman.

4. For arms, overlap ends of chenille stem ½" and glue together to form a loop. With overlap at back of neck, glue arms to snowman. Glue star and heart cutouts to front of arms.

5. For scarf, fringe ends of 5½" ribbon length approx. ⅛". Knot scarf around neck.

6. For hat, glue spool to center of circle cutout; glue 2½" ribbon length around hat for hatband. Glue hat to head.

7. For hanger, glue ends of remaining ribbon into hole at top of spool.

ENCHANTING ORNAMENTS

Using your favorite holiday molds, you can craft enchanting paper ornaments like these. The shapes can be painted any way you like! We glued our Santa face, teddy bear, and Christmas tree to fabric-covered poster board bases, then trimmed them with gold cord.

PAPER ART ORNAMENTS

For each ornament, you will need a plastic, metal, or clay mold; Creative Paperclay™ (available at craft stores); a white paper towel; fabric and poster board for background; paper-backed fusible web; 1/8" dia. gold twisted cord; desired colors of acrylic paint; small paintbrushes; matte clear acrylic spray; and a low-temperature hot glue gun and glue sticks.

1. Wet paper towel and lay towel loosely over mold. Firmly press Creative Paperclay™ into mold.
2. If using a plastic mold, allow shape to dry in mold approx. 24 hours. If using a metal or clay mold, preheat oven to 350 degrees, place mold on cookie sheet in oven, and immediately turn off oven; after 20 minutes, remove mold from oven and allow to cool.
3. Gently remove shape from mold and allow to dry completely on a flat surface. Trim excess paper towel from shape.
4. Paint shape as desired; allow to dry.
5. Allowing to dry after each coat, apply 2 coats of acrylic spray to shape.
6. For background, follow manufacturer's instructions to fuse web to wrong side of

fabric. Remove paper backing and fuse fabric to poster board. Glue molded paper shape to fabric-covered poster board. Cut out background in desired shape (for our Santa, we cut a square from background and cut notches in edges; for our tree, we trimmed background close to sides and top of tree, cut a block under tree for base, and glued another strip of fabric along top of block for trim; for our bear, we trimmed background to approx. 1/4" from bear).
7. (*Note:* Before cutting cord, apply glue to cord around area to be cut.) For trim, glue cord to ornament as desired.
8. For hanger, knot ends of a 6" length of cord together; glue knot to top back of ornament.

PLAYFUL PENGUINS

*F*ashioned from crafting foam, these precious Santa penguins are super projects for kids! The foam cutouts are simply glued together, and facial features are added with dimensional paint. Button accents finish the playful pair.

PLAYFUL PENGUINS

Note: These ornaments were designed to be fun and easy for children to make. For young children, you may want to cut out the pieces so the ornaments will be ready to assemble.

For each penguin, you will need white, red, and black 1/16" thick crafting foam; three 3/8" dia. buttons; white and orange dimensional paint; tracing paper; and a low-temperature hot glue gun and glue sticks.

1. Trace patterns, page 118, onto tracing paper; cut out.
2. Use patterns to cut body from black foam; hat from red foam; and hat trim, pom-pom, and chest from white foam.
3. Center hat at top of body with straight edges of pieces touching. Center and glue hat trim over touching edges of hat and body. Glue pom-pom to hat, chest to body, and buttons to chest.
4. For face, use white paint to paint eyes and orange paint to paint nose. Allow to dry.

ELEGANT ACCENTS

*S*teeped in elegance, this timeless collection offers an opulent array of Yuletide ornaments. Every trim is tastefully designed using luxurious materials and exquisite details. From dazzling to divine, there are fanciful embellishments for celebrating in grand style. Shown here, the gilded silk poinsettias and stunning tassels shimmering amid the tree lights are just a hint of the majestic adornments you'll discover in this beautiful treasury.

TOUCHED WITH GOLD

GILDED POINSETTIAS

For each poinsettia, you will need an approx. 6" dia. silk poinsettia, 3 silk holly leaves removed from stems, gold craft foil and craft foil adhesive (we used Liquid BEADS™ Press & Peel Foil and Dimensional Bond), metallic gold acrylic paint, small paintbrush, corrugated cardboard, straight pins, and a hot glue gun and glue sticks.

1. Remove poinsettia petal sections from stem.
2. Place petal sections and holly leaves right side up on cardboard and stretch flat, pinning in place.
3. Follow manufacturer's instructions to apply an approx. 1/4"w stripe of craft foil along edges of each petal and leaf.
4. Replace petal sections on poinsettia stem. With half of each leaf showing, glue holly leaves to backs of petals.
5. Use paintbrush to paint stamens gold; allow to dry.

ELEGANT TASSELS

For each tassel, you will need 1 1/2 skeins of embroidery floss (for our red and green tassels, we used 3/4 skein each of red and green), 14 yds of heavy gold thread, and 14" of 1/16" dia. gold cord for hanger.

1. Cut floss apart at ends of each skein (Fig. 1); remove labels from skein. Cut approx. 75 lengths of gold thread same length as floss (approx. 6 1/2"). Mix floss and thread lengths together.

Fig. 1

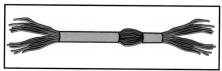

2. For hanger, knot cord around center of floss and thread bundle. Knot and fray each end of cord.
3. Either fold floss and thread bundle in half or twist bundle at center and then fold in half (we twisted our red tassels, but not our red and green tassels). Wrap remaining gold thread 5 to 10 times around tassel approx. 1/2" from top and knot ends together to secure; trim ends approx. 1/4" from knot and tuck ends under wrapped thread.
4. Trim ends of tassel even.
5. To hang tassel, tie ends of hanger around tree branch.

*I*nspired by the elegance of their larger counterparts, these miniature topiaries are fashioned from plastic foam balls and a papier-mâché star. The balls are decorated with holly or velvet poinsettia petals, and the star is covered with moss and wrapped with gold cord. The festive fancies are displayed in small moss-filled wire baskets finished with gilded bows.

MINIATURE TOPIARIES

For each topiary, you will need a 2"h wire basket, floral foam to fit in basket, large cinnamon stick for trunk, metallic gold spray paint, sheet moss, 1/2 yd of 1"w wired ribbon, 6" of clear nylon thread, and a hot glue gun and glue sticks.
For holly topiary, you will *also* need a 2" dia. plastic foam ball and small silk holly sprigs with berries.
For poinsettia topiary, you will *also* need a 2" dia. plastic foam ball, two approx. 6" dia. wired velvet poinsettias, and wire cutters.
For star topiary, you will *also* need a 4"w papier-mâché star, 1 1/3 yd of 1/8" dia. gold twisted cord, foam brush, and craft glue.

LITTLE TOPIARIES

HOLLY TOPIARY

1. For trunk, spray paint cinnamon stick gold; allow to dry.
2. Insert 1 end of cinnamon stick into foam ball; glue to secure.
3. Glue holly sprigs to ball, covering ball completely.
4. Glue moss to foam piece, covering foam completely; glue foam piece into basket. Insert remaining end of cinnamon stick into foam in basket.
5. Beginning and ending at front of topiary, weave ribbon through top edge of basket. Tie ribbon ends into a bow; trim ends.
6. For hanger, knot ends of nylon thread together; hot glue knot to top of topiary.

POINSETTIA TOPIARY

1. Follow Steps 1 and 2 of Holly Topiary instructions.
2. Leaving stems attached to petals, remove petals and stamens from poinsettias. Leaving an approx. 1/4" dia. space at top of ball, glue larger petals to foam ball, covering ball completely. Insert stems of smaller petals into top of ball; shape petals around ball and glue in place if necessary. Insert stamens into top of ball and glue in place if necessary.
3. To complete ornament, follow Steps 4 - 6 of Holly Topiary instructions.

STAR TOPIARY

1. Follow Step 1 of Holly Topiary instructions. Hot glue 1 end of cinnamon stick to 1 side (back) of star.
2. Use foam brush to apply a coat of craft glue to star; cover star with moss and allow to dry. If necessary, trim moss to retain star shape.
3. Wrap cord around star as desired; hot glue ends to back of star to secure.
4. To complete ornament, follow Steps 4 - 6 of Holly Topiary instructions.

PEARLS ALL AROUND

*T*his precious gem of
an ornament is simple to
make using a plastic foam
ball. Wrapped in satin cord
and a string of small pearls,
it's topped with an ivory
bow and has a loop of pearls
for the hanger.

SATIN CORD BALL

You will need a 3" dia. plastic foam ball,
2⅝ yds of ½" dia. twisted satin cord,
2¾ yds of 4mm pearl garland, 13" of
1⅜"w wired satin ribbon, jewel glue,
and a hot glue gun and glue sticks.

1. Tucking ends of cord under wrapped
cord at top and bottom of foam ball,
wrap cord around ball, covering ball
completely and hot gluing cord in place
as you go.
2. Beginning at bottom of ball, use jewel
glue to glue pearl garland along edges of
cord. Allow to dry.
3. For hanger, fold remaining length of
pearl garland in half to form a loop; hot
glue ends to top of ball. Tie ribbon
length into a bow; trim ends. Hot glue
bow to top of ball, covering ends
of hanger.

TIMEWORN ROSES

*F*ashioned from bleached strips of luxurious velvet, our timeworn roses will add an elegant touch to packages, the tree, and more. The blooms are so easy to make that you'll want to craft a whole bouquet of these resplendent beauties!

VELVET ROSES

For several roses and rosebuds, you will need 1/3 yd of 40"w 100% rayon velvet, thread to match velvet, velvet leaves, bleach, small glass container for bleaching velvet (we used a 2-cup measuring cup), liquid fray preventative, craft stick, and a hot glue gun and glue sticks.

1. (*Caution:* Wear rubber gloves and work in a well-ventilated area when working with bleach.) Crumple velvet and place in container. Pour a small amount of bleach onto velvet. Briefly allow velvet to absorb bleach (bleaching time will vary depending on color of velvet and desired effect). Using craft stick to turn velvet, pour additional bleach onto velvet a small amount at a time. Remove velvet from container to determine if more bleaching is desired. Repeat bleaching process if desired. Rinse velvet thoroughly with cool water and allow to dry.

2. For each large rose, cut a 34" long strip of velvet that tapers from 3" to 4" in width. For each medium rose, cut a 21" long strip that tapers from 3" to 4" in width. For each rosebud, cut a 10" long strip that tapers from 2" to 3" in width. Apply fray preventative to edges of velvet strips; allow to dry.

3. (*Note:* Follow remaining steps for each rose or rosebud.) Matching wrong sides and long edges, fold velvet strip in half. Using a 1/4" seam allowance, baste long edges together. To form center of rose, knot narrow end of velvet strip. Pull basting thread to gather strip. Knot and trim basting thread. Wind strip loosely around knot, tacking bottom edge (gathered edge) of strip to knot to secure. To form petals, continue to wind strip around center with bottom edge winding slightly downward and tacking bottom edge in place as you go. At end of strip, fold raw edges 1/4" to wrong side and stitch in place.

4. Glue stems of leaves to bottom of rose.

PAPER PRETTIES

MARBLEIZED PAPER BOW AND GIFT BAG

Crafted from handmade or purchased marbleized paper, these handsome decorations have classic style. The bow is embellished with a pretty pearl button, and the gift bag holds a bouquet of greenery, berries, and poinsettias.

You will need a hot glue gun and glue sticks and either purchased marbleized paper or the following items: 8½" x 11" sheets of lightweight watercolor paper, 1 gallon of liquid starch, a 9" x 18" disposable aluminum foil roasting pan, several colors of acrylic paint (we used white, red, green, and metallic gold), paper towels, and waxed paper.

For each bow, you will *also* need metallic gold spray paint, a ⅞" dia. pearl button, and tracing paper.

For each gift bag, you will *also* need a 2" square of 1" thick plastic foam, assorted small silk flowers and greenery with berries, a miniature present, two 6" lengths of ⅛"w gold flat cord, and a ⅛" hole punch.

Note: If using purchased marbleized paper, follow Bow or Gift Bag instructions. If marbleizing paper, follow Marbleizing Paper instructions first.

MARBLEIZING PAPER

1. Pour starch into pan to a depth of 1".
2. (*Note:* Repeat Steps 2 - 6 as necessary to marbleize desired amount of paper. Apply fresh paint to starch for each sheet of paper.) To apply paint to starch surface, hold bottle of paint near surface and gently squeeze out a small dot of paint (paint will float and begin to spread). Repeat to apply several dots of each color of paint. Use a fingertip or the corner of a paper towel to remove dots that do not spread.
3. To form marble design, use a fork or the wooden end of a paintbrush to swirl paint around on surface of starch, forming desired patterns.
4. Gently place white paper on starch surface (paper will float); immediately pick up paper by 2 corners and lay paper paint side up on a layer of paper towels. Use dry paper towels to blot excess starch and paint from paper. Lay paper on waxed paper; allow to dry.
5. After marbleizing paper, remove any excess paint from starch in pan by placing a layer of paper towels on starch surface. Lift towels from starch and discard.
6. Use a warm, dry iron to press marbleized paper.

BOW

1. Spray wrong side of marbleized paper with gold paint; allow to dry.
2. Use bow and streamers patterns, page 119, and follow *Tracing Patterns*, page 126.
3. Use patterns to cut shapes from paper.
4. With wrong side (gold side) of bow shape facing up, fold ends of bow to center and overlap ½", creasing loops slightly at outer edges; glue to secure. Glue button to center of bow, covering ends of paper. Glue streamers to back of bow.

GIFT BAG

1. Cut a 4" x 7" piece from marbleized paper.
2. Center and glue foam piece to wrong side of paper piece. Fold short edges of paper piece over foam; glue in place. For bottom of bag, fold edges of paper at 1 end of wrapped foam piece gift-wrap style and glue to secure.
3. For handles, use hole punch to punch 2 holes approx. 1" apart approx. ¼" from top edge on front and back of bag. Thread 1 cord length through holes on front of bag and knot each end inside bag. Repeat with remaining cord length for handle on back of bag.
4. Arrange flowers and greenery in bag; glue to secure if necessary. Glue miniature present to greenery.

NOBLE NUTCRACKER

Standing at attention, our noble nutcracker will guard your tree in grand style. Fabric appliqués are fused to poster board for the fanciful fellow. Details are added with a black felt-tip pen and gold glitter paint.

NUTCRACKER

You will need white, yellow, peach, red, blue, and black fabrics for appliqués; paper-backed fusible web; poster board; gold glitter paint; small paintbrush; peach and red colored pencils; 3/16" dia. red wooden bead; craft knife and cutting mat; black permanent felt-tip pen with fine point; 6" of clear nylon thread for hanger; and a hot glue gun and glue sticks.

1. For appliqués, trace patterns, page 119, separately onto tracing paper; cut out. Fuse web to wrong sides of appliqué fabrics. Use patterns to cut shapes from fabrics.
2. Remove paper backing from appliqués. Place face and beard appliqué right side up over pattern. Use black pen to trace face and mustache onto shape and outline edges of hair and beard.

3. Referring to pattern for placement, arrange appliqués on poster board, overlapping appliqués as necessary; fuse in place.
4. Use craft knife to cut ornament from poster board.
5. Use black pen to draw fringe on epaulets, buttons on coat, and a line down center of pants. Use colored

pencils to color face peach and cheeks red.
6. Use paintbrush to apply gold paint to crown, epaulets, fringe on epaulets, buttons, and belt buckle; allow to dry.
7. Glue bead to top of crown.
8. For hanger, knot ends of nylon thread together; glue knot to top back of nutcracker.

STARRY SNOWFLAKES

S tar-shaped snowflakes are cut from foam core board and dipped in plaster of paris to craft these pristine trims. For a shimmering effect, iridescent glitter paint is added to the edges, and dimensional paint creates an embossed look.

DIMENSIONAL SNOWFLAKES

For each snowflake, you will need 1/4" thick foam core board, plaster of paris, white gesso, snow white Tulip® Colorpoint® Puff Stitch Paint, satin-finish white acrylic spray paint, iridescent glitter liquid acrylic paint, small flat paintbrush, foam brush, craft knife and cutting mat, 7" of 1/8"w white satin ribbon for hanger, floral wire, wire cutters, tracing paper, fine sandpaper, and a hot glue gun and glue sticks.

1. Use desired pattern, page 120, and follow *Tracing Patterns*, page 126. Use pattern and craft knife to cut snowflake from foam core board.
2. To make a temporary hanger for dipping snowflake in plaster, cut a 15" length of wire. Bend wire into a "U" shape; bend approx. 1" at each end of wire in at a right angle and press ends into 2 opposite edges of snowflake (Fig. 1).

Fig. 1

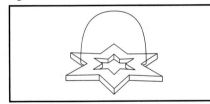

3. Follow manufacturer's instructions to mix plaster of paris in a large disposable baking pan (plaster should fill pan to a depth of at least 1/2"). Quickly dip snowflake in plaster and shake off excess. Hang snowflake over a protected surface and allow plaster to set (when set, plaster will be cool to the touch). Remove temporary hanger from snowflake.
4. Use sandpaper to gently smooth plaster drips from bottom of snowflake.

5. Use foam brush to apply gesso to snowflake; allow to dry.
6. (*Note:* Allow to dry after each paint step.) Use stitch paint to paint dots and lines as desired on top (front) of snowflake. Follow manufacturer's instructions to expand paint.
7. Spray paint snowflake white.
8. Use flat paintbrush to paint edges of snowflake with iridescent paint.
9. For hanger, fold ribbon in half and glue ends to top back of snowflake.

ANGELS DIVINE

Using photocopies of our vintage angel art, you can easily craft this heavenly host of ornaments. Golden wired ribbon, trims, and charms adorn the padded decorations.

HEIRLOOM ANGEL ORNAMENTS

For each ornament, you will need cream-colored fabric for front and back of ornament; lightweight cardboard; low-loft polyester bonded batting; disappearing ink fabric marking pen; tracing paper; hot glue gun and glue sticks; and either a photocopy transfer of desired ornament design, page 121, (made at copy shops) or a standard photocopy of desired design and the following items: transfer medium for fabric (transfers photocopies to fabric; available at craft stores) and foam brushes.

For oval ornament, you will *also* need 13" of 1¼"w wired ribbon, 13" of ⅛" dia. gold cording with ¼"w flange, 7" of ⅛" dia. gold twisted cord, and a 2" long tassel.

For round ornament, you will *also* need 16" of 1⅜"w wired ribbon, 16" of 1"w gold wired ribbon, 14" of ½"w gold gimp trim, 5" of ⅛" dia. gold twisted cord, and a 2" long gold fleur-de-lis charm.

For rectangular ornament, you will *also* need 19" of 5/16"w gold flat trim, 21" of 2¼"w wired ribbon, 9" of ⅛" dia. gold twisted cord, and a 7/8"w gold heart charm.

1. Trace background pattern for desired ornament (shown in blue), page 121, onto tracing paper; cut out. Use pattern to cut 1 shape each from fabric (ornament back), batting, and cardboard. For ornament front, cut a fabric piece approx. 1" larger on all sides than pattern.

2. (*Note:* If using a photocopy transfer, follow Steps 2 and 4 - 8. If using a standard photocopy and transfer medium, follow Steps 3 - 8.) Place ornament front fabric piece right side up on a hard protected surface. Cutting close to design, cut out transfer (be sure to cut away background pattern, shown in blue). Center transfer design side down on fabric. Using a hot, dry iron, firmly press transfer for 8 to 10 seconds; allow to cool. Remove transfer paper from design.

3. Cutting close to design, cut out photocopy (be sure to cut away background pattern, shown in blue). Follow transfer medium manufacturer's instructions to transfer design to center of ornament front fabric piece.

4. (*Note:* Use hot glue for remaining steps.) Center batting, then cardboard on wrong side of ornament front fabric piece. At approx. ½" intervals, make clips in fabric to approx. ⅛" from cardboard shape. Alternating sides and pulling fabric taut, glue edges of fabric to cardboard.

5. (*Note:* For remaining steps, before cutting cording or cord, apply glue to ½" around area to be cut and then cut.) For trim on oval ornament, begin at top of ornament and glue flange of cording along edges on back of ornament. Glue hanging loop of tassel to center bottom on back of ornament. For hanger, fold cord in half and glue ends to top back of ornament. Tie ribbon into a bow; trim ends. Glue bow to top of ornament.

6. For trim on round ornament, begin at top of ornament and glue gimp trim along edges on back of ornament with half of trim extending beyond edges of ornament. For hanger, fold 1⅜"w ribbon in half. Twist ribbon approx. 1¾" from fold; glue twist at top of ornament for loop. Glue streamers to back of ornament and trim ends. Thread cord through ribbon loop at top of ornament and glue ends to back of charm. Tie 1"w ribbon into a bow; trim ends. Glue bow to top of ornament.

7. For trim on rectangular ornament, glue lengths of gold flat trim approx. ⅛" inside edges on front of ornament. For hanger, glue 1 end of cord to each top corner on back of ornament. Tie ribbon into a bow; trim ends. Glue bow to top right corner of ornament. Glue charm to bow.

8. Glue ornament back fabric piece to back of ornament.

VELVET BEAUTIES

*E*xquisitely embellished
u   beads, jewels, and other
o   ent trims, miniature
v   t stockings and a
r   cross make grand
o   ments for the evergreen.
T   lush red fabric makes
a   iking contrast to
t   ree's green boughs!

ADED VELVET STOCKINGS

each stocking, you will need red
   vet, thread to match velvet, 6" of ¹/₂"w
   tallic gold gimp trim, 6" of ¹/₈" dia.
   d twisted cord, gold seed beads
   pprox. 134 are needed for bow design
   d 109 for snowflake design), 6mm
   ld bugle beads (47 are needed for
   w design and 24 for snowflake
   sign), beading needle, gold thread, 7"

of ¹/₂"w satin ribbon to match velvet for
facing at top of stocking, fabric marking
pen, tweezers (if needed), pressing
cloth, tissue paper, and tracing paper.

1. Trace stocking pattern onto tracing
paper; cut out. Use fabric marking
pen to draw around pattern twice (once
in reverse) on wrong side of velvet.
Cutting ¹/₂" outside drawn lines, cut out
stocking shapes.
2. Trace desired beading pattern,
page 122, onto tissue paper. Center
pattern approx. 1¹/₂" from top edge on
right side of 1 stocking piece (front);
pin or baste in place.
3. Refer to Beading Key, page 122, to
sew beads to stocking piece over
pattern. Using tweezers if necessary,
carefully tear pattern away from
beaded design.
4. Pin stocking pieces right sides
together. Using a ¹/₂" seam allowance
and leaving top edge open, sew shapes
together. Trim seam allowance to ¹/₄"
and clip seam allowance at curves; turn
stocking right side out.
5. Using pressing cloth, lightly press
stocking; press top edge of stocking ¹/₂"
to wrong side.
6. For hanger, knot ends of cord
together. Place knot just inside top of
stocking at heel side seamline; tack
in place.
7. For facing at top of stocking, press 1
end of ribbon length ¹/₂" to 1 side
(wrong side). Matching 1 long edge of
ribbon to top edge of stocking, place
ribbon in stocking, overlapping pressed
end over unpressed end. Whipstitch
ribbon in place along top edge of
stocking.
8. With 1 edge of gimp trim extending
approx. ¹/₈" beyond top edge of stocking
and overlapping ends at back, sew gimp
trim along top edge of stocking.

APPLIQUÉD VELVET CROSS

You will need red velvet; metallic gold
fabric for appliqué; lightweight fabric to
match velvet for backing; paper-backed
fusible web; low-loft polyester bonded
batting; lightweight cardboard;
iridescent gold dimensional fabric paint;
¹/₂ yd of ¹/₈" dia. and 8" of ¹/₁₆" dia. gold
twisted cord; one 15mm oval, one
15mm round, and four 14mm teardrop
red acrylic jewels; jewel glue; pressing
cloth; fabric marking pen; tracing paper;
and a hot glue gun and glue sticks.

1. Trace large cross pattern onto tracing
paper; cut out. Use pattern to cut 1
shape each from batting, cardboard, and
backing fabric. Use fabric marking pen
to draw around pattern on wrong side
of velvet; cut out shape 1" outside
drawn lines.
2. Use small cross pattern and follow
Making Appliqués, page 126, to make
cross appliqué from gold fabric. Remove
paper backing. Center appliqué on right
side of velvet cross and use pressing
cloth to fuse in place.
3. Center batting, then cardboard shape
on wrong side of velvet cross. At ¹/₂"
intervals, make clips in velvet to approx.
¹/₈" from cardboard shape. Alternating
sides and pulling fabric taut, hot glue
edges of fabric to cardboard.
4. Use gold paint to paint along edges of
cross appliqué, covering raw edges of
fabric; allow to dry.
5. Use jewel glue to glue jewels to cross
appliqué; allow to dry.
6. (*Note:* Before cutting cord, apply glue
to ¹/₂" of cord around area to be cut and
then cut cord.) For trim, hot glue
¹/₈" dia. cord along edges of velvet cross.
For hanger, fold ¹/₁₆" dia. cord in half.
Hot glue ends to top back of cross.
7. Hot glue backing fabric piece to back
of cross.

ELEGANT TOUCH

A plain glass ball is enhanced with a gold sponge-painted poinsettia for stunning results. Gold foil accents elegantly outline the favorite Christmas flower.

SPONGE-PAINTED POINSETTIA ORNAMENT

You will need a 4" dia. red matte glass ball ornament, metallic gold acrylic paint, metallic gold spray paint (if needed), gold craft foil and craft foil adhesive (we used Liquid BEADS™ Press & Peel Foil and Dimensional Bond), Miracle® sponges (dry compressed sponges available at craft stores), paper towel, tracing paper, and matte clear acrylic spray.

1. Apply 1 coat of acrylic spray to ball; allow to dry.
2. Remove cap and hanger from ball. Spray paint cap gold if necessary; allow to dry and set aside.
3. Trace petal pattern onto tracing paper; cut out. Use pattern to cut petal shape from dry sponge.
4. (*Note:* Use a glass or cup with an opening slightly smaller than ornament to hold ornament while working.) Dip dampened sponge shape in acrylic paint; do not saturate. Remove excess paint on a paper towel. Keeping sponge level, lightly press sponge on ball to paint 1 petal; carefully lift sponge. Leaving an approx. $^1/_2$" dia. space at center and overlapping petals as desired, repeat to stamp poinsettia on ball (we stamped 10 petals to form our poinsettia). Allow to dry.

5. Follow manufacturer's instructions to apply craft foil at center of poinsettia to make stamens and along edges of petals.
6. Allowing to dry between coats, spray ornament with 2 coats of acrylic spray.
7. Replace cap and hanger on ornament.

REGAL RIBBON ANGEL

...ttire of our
...ngel is fashioned
...ths of elegant
...on. She holds a
...r in her delicate
...hands, and her
...d is crowned
...o of gold cord.

...F GOLD

...ed a 1⅝"h porcelain angel
..." long arms (available in sets
...es), 10½" of 5"w wired
...dress, 21" of 2⅝"w wired
...shawl, 16" of 2½"w wired
...wings, 4" of ¹/₁₆" dia. gold
...for halo, 1⅛"w star
.../₂" of floral wire, and a hot
...d glue sticks.

..., overlap ends of 5"w ribbon
..." to form a tube. Glue ends
...overlap to secure. Gather 1
...around neck of angel head;
...re.

...l, gather center of 2⅝"w
...een fingers; glue center of
...ack of angel's neck. Cross
...s loosely at front of angel and
...d sides to back, forming
...; glue to secure. Arrange
...trim ends as desired.

3. Glue arms to wrong side of bottom edge of shawl. Glue star appliqué between hands.

4. For wings, gather center of 2½"w ribbon between fingers and glue center of ribbon to back of angel's neck. Arrange ribbon and trim ends as desired.

5. For halo, form cord into an approx. 1" dia. circle with a ¾" stem; glue stem to back of angel's head.

6. For hanger, bend wire in half to form a loop; glue ends to top back of ornament.

SHIMMERING SMOCKED BALL

Delicate pleats and geometric stitches embellish this beautiful smocked tree-trimmer. The simple pattern makes it easy to smock, and metallic threads provide a rich shimmer. Featuring a lush tassel and a wired-ribbon bow, the ornament is sure to become a cherished keepsake.

SMOCKED ORNAMENT

You will need 10-row pleated 44/45"w white broadcloth (includes holding rows), gold (002) and red (003) Kreinik® fine (#8) braid, 13" of 3/16" dia. metallic gold twisted cord, 5" of 1/4"w gold flat trim, 3½" long white tassel with hanging loop removed, 12" of 1½"w white wired ribbon, 3/4" dia. white wooden bead, 2½" dia. plastic foam ball, size 7 crewel needle, white sewing thread, blocking board (optional), stainless steel pins, and a hot glue gun and glue sticks.

1. (*Note:* Refer to chart and Smocking instructions, page 65, and follow Steps 1 - 6 to smock pleated panel for ornament. Use 1 strand of braid for all smocking. Finished length of smocked area should be 9". We stitched 40 repeats across our panel.) Using red braid and beginning with an up cable, work Cable Stitch across rows 2 and 8.

2. Using gold braid for Outline Stitch and red braid for Stem Stitch, work Wheat Stitch across row 3.

3. Using red braid for Outline Stitch and gold braid for Stem Stitch, work Wheat Stitch across row 7.

4. Using red braid and beginning with a down cable, work 1 space/1 step Wave Stitch between rows 4 and 5.

5. Using red braid and beginning with an up cable, work 1 space/1 step Wave Stitch between rows 5 and 6.

6. Using gold braid, work 3 Satin Stitches between each pair of Wave Stitches across row 5.

l but top and bottom
eads (holding rows). To
d panel, place panel right
n blocking board or ironing
end of panel in place. Using
king board or an artists'
ep panel straight, arrange
and stretch panel gently as
til smocked area measures
remaining edges of panel in
ron on steam setting, hold
1" above panel and steam
panel is slightly damp.
to dry. Remove panel from
rd or ironing board.
ful not to cut gathering
short edges of panel to
from smocked area.
rt edge of panel 1/2" to
Beginning with unfolded
rap panel around foam
ping short edges and
cking stitches; pin in place
be at back of ornament).
ering threads at top and
nel until panel fits snugly
knot and trim thread ends.
trim excess fabric at top
of ornament so edges lie
all. Glue top and bottom
to ball. Whipstitch edges of
er at back of ornament.
.
efore cutting cord, apply
f cord around area to be cut
cord.) Glue tassel to bottom
. Glue a length of cord
of tassel. Glue a length of flat
tassel binding.
er, glue ends of remaining
into bead. Glue bead to top
. Glue remaining flat trim
om of bead.
on length into a bow; trim
ow to ornament.

SMOCKING CHART

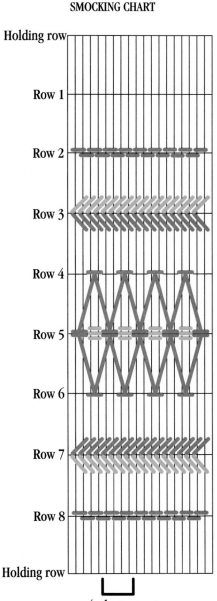

Holding row

Row 1

Row 2

Row 3

Row 4

Row 5

Row 6

Row 7

Row 8

Holding row

4-pleat repeat

SMOCKING

Smocking is worked on pleated fabric. Most fabric stores that sell smocking supplies will also pleat fabric.

Smocking designs are worked from left to right using the gathering threads in the pleated panel as guidelines for stitching. In the chart these threads are indicated by horizontal lines and are numbered as "rows." Each vertical line in the chart represents the top of 1 pleat.

For each stitch, the needle is usually inserted horizontally through about the top 1/3 of the pleat parallel to the gathering threads. When making a stitch, the thread should be pulled so that each stitch is snug but does not distort the shape of the pleat.

To begin a row of smocking, thread crewel needle and knot end of thread. Leaving at least 2 or 3 pleats unsmocked at each end of panel, bring needle up through left side of first pleat to be stitched.

To end a row of smocking, complete last stitch and take needle down through valley between the last 2 stitched pleats. Take a small stitch in same pleat on back of panel behind smocked area; knot and trim thread.

Cable Stitch: A row of Cable Stitch consists of alternating up and down Cable Stitches. For an *up* Cable Stitch (Fig. 1), bring needle up at 1; keeping thread *above* needle, take needle through second pleat at 2. For a *down* Cable Stitch (Fig. 2, page 66), take needle through third pleat at 3, keeping thread *below* needle. Repeat, alternating up and down Cable Stitches. The up and down stitches in a row should touch (Fig. 3, page 66).

Fig. 1

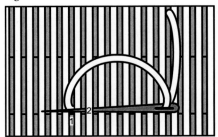

Continued on page 66

Fig. 2

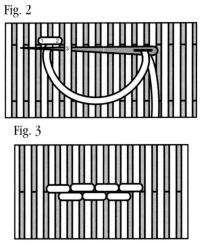

Fig. 3

Wheat Stitch: A row of Wheat Stitch consists of 1 row of Outline Stitch and 1 row of Stem Stitch (instructions follow) worked very closely together so that they touch each other and resemble a stalk of wheat (Fig. 4).

Fig. 4

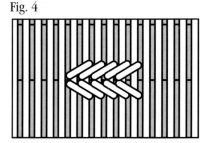

Outline Stitch: Keeping thread *above* needle, bring needle up through left side of first pleat and through second pleat as if to make an up Cable Stitch. Repeat (Fig. 5).

Fig. 5

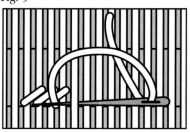

Stem Stitch: Keeping thread *below* needle, bring needle up through left side of first pleat and through second pleat as if to make a down Cable Stitch. Repeat (Fig. 6).

Fig. 6

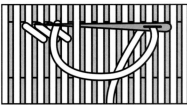

Wave, or Trellis Stitch: The size of a Wave Stitch is determined by spaces (the number of rows spanned) and steps (how many stitches are in each "leg" of the wave). These instructions are for a 1 space/1 step Wave Stitch. A Wave Stitch is a combination of level and step stitches. The level stitches are worked like up or down Cable Stitches. For a row of Wave Stitches that point up (shown on chart between Rows 4 and 5), begin with a down Cable Stitch. For "step-up" stitch (Fig. 7), take needle through next pleat at 3. For top level stitch, work an up Cable Stitch. For "step-down" stitch (Fig. 8), take needle through next pleat at 5. Repeat. For a row of Wave Stitches that point down (shown on chart between Rows 5 and 6), begin with an up Cable Stitch and work "step-down" and "step-up" stitches in the same manner as for an up-pointing row of stitches; for bottom level stitches, work down Cable Stitches (Fig. 9).

Fig. 7

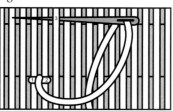

Fig. 8

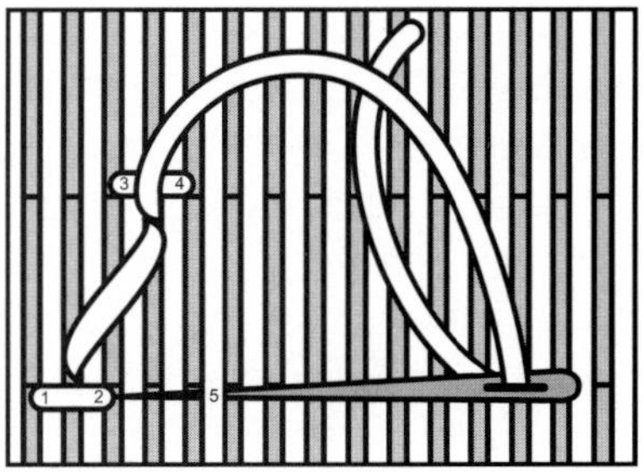

Fig. 9

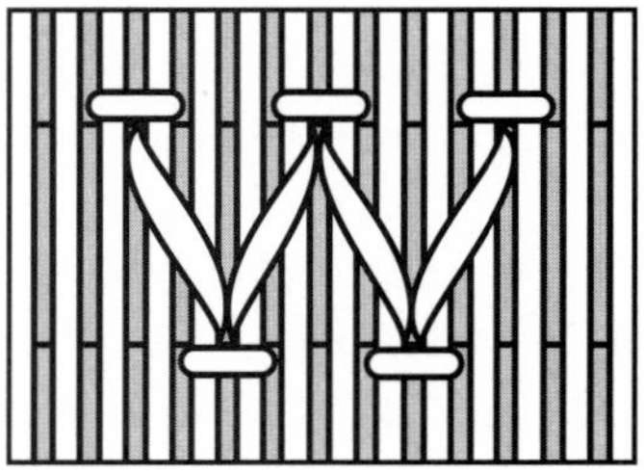

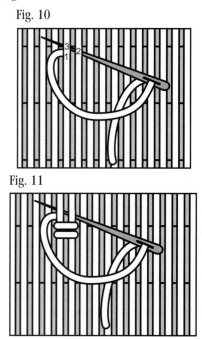

Satin Stitch: For this stitch, insert needle through pleats at a slight angle to keep stitches horizontal. Come up at 1 (Fig. 10); take needle through second pleat at 2 and through first pleat again at 3. With stitches touching, repeat (Fig. 11).

Fig. 10

Fig. 11

SEASON'S GREETINGS

photocopies
...letide postcards
...etings that
...d over the years
...delightful
...Embellished
...ily cutouts
...nciful trims,
...d party cracker
...will lend a
...uch to the
...ft packages.

... FANS

...you will need either a
...measures at least 4" x 6"
...otocopy of one, white
...a 4" dia. gold doily, 1/2 yd
...gimp trim, tracing paper,
...t, and a hot glue gun and

...cement to glue card to

...tern, page 122, and follow
...erns, page 126. Use pattern
...pe from covered

...ieces from edge of doily.
...3/4" of doily pieces
...yond edges of fan, hot glue
...doily pieces along edges on
...fan.
...mp trim along edges of fan,
...pprox. 3/4" loop at center

CHRISTMAS CRACKER

You will need a 5" x 11" fabric piece, a 6" length cut from an approx. 1¹/4" dia. cardboard wrapping paper tube, either a postcard that measures at least 2" x 5" or a color photocopy of one, a 4" dia. gold doily, two 5" lengths of ³/16"w gold gimp trim, two 12" lengths of ¹/16" dia. gold twisted cord, hot glue gun and glue sticks, and desired favor to fit in cracker (optional).

1. Center tube along 1 long edge of fabric. Roll fabric around tube; glue overlapped edge to secure.

2. Knot 1 length of cord around fabric at 1 end of tube; knot and fray ends of cord. If desired, place favor in cracker. Tie remaining end of cracker with remaining cord length.
3. Spot glue doily to center front of cracker.
4. Cut a 2" x 5" piece from card. Center and glue card piece over doily on cracker, overlapping ends.
5. Beginning and ending at back of cracker, glue gimp trim lengths along top and bottom edges of card strip.

67

NATIVITY SAMPLERS

Cross stitched to resemble traditional samplers, these miniature pillow ornaments will be treasured for many years to come. Each features an inspirational passage from the Nativity story.

NATIVITY ORNAMENTS

For each ornament, you will need two 9" squares of raw Belfast Linen (32 ct), embroidery floss (see color key, page 69), thread to match linen, lightweight fusible interfacing, polyester fiberfill, fabric marking pencil, and 4" of 4-ply jute for hanger.

1. Using 2 strands of floss for Cross Stitch, follow *Cross Stitch* and *Working on Linen* instructions, pages 126 and 127, to work desired ornament design, page 69, over 2 fabric threads on 1 fabric square.
2. Follow manufacturer's instructions to fuse interfacing to wrong side of stitched piece. Use fabric marking pencil to lightly mark edges of stitched design on interfaced side of stitched piece.
3. Place stitched piece and remaining fabric piece right sides together. Using a short stitch length and leaving an opening for turning, sew fabric pieces together approx. 3/8" from stitched

design, following contours of stitched design. Trim seam allowance to 1/4". Clip curves and corners. Turn right side out and press. Lightly stuff ornament with fiberfill; sew final closure by hand.

4. Use 2 strands of embroidery floss to work Blanket Stitch, page 127, along edges of ornament.
5. For hanger, fold jute in half and tack ends to center top on back of ornament.

ORNAMENTS

ANC.	COLOR
2	white
878	green
877	lt green
900	grey
891	yellow
890	dk yellow
944	brown
897	dk red
1035	blue
1033	lt blue
847	lt grey
778	lt peach

43w x 50h

We are come to worship Him

41w x 51h

42w x 50h

Glory to God in the highest

69

NOSTALGIC NOEL

A fairy-tale Christmas can be yours with the fanciful forget-me-nots and sentimental sweethearts in this collection of Victorian ornaments. Embellished with lace, ribbons, and charms, these lovely trims — from the beaded icicles to the dried flower bouquets — are rich in romance. You'll fall in love with the tiny crocheted angels and shimmering snowflakes shown here. Worked in cotton thread, the Yuletide dainties dance and drift across the evergreen's branches. With these nostalgic offerings, you can have a holiday that others only dream about!

ANGELS IN THE SNOW

CROCHETED CLOTHESPIN ANGELS

Finished Size: 4" h

MATERIALS (for 1 angel)
Bedspread Weight Cotton Thread
    (size 10), approx. 45 yards
Steel crochet hook, size 6 (1.80 mm) *or*
    size needed for gauge
Finishing supplies: 3¾" Round, slotted
    clothespin; craft glue; 8" of ⅛"w satin
    ribbon for bow; and 8" of clear nylon
    thread for hanger

ABBREVIATIONS

ch(s)	chain(s)
dc	double crochet(s)
hdc	half double crochet(s)
mm	millimeters
Rnd(s)	Round(s)
sc	single crochet(s)
sp(s)	space(s)
st(s)	stitch(es)
YO	yarn over

★ — work instructions following ★ as
many *more* times as indicated in
addition to the first time.

† to † — work all instructions from
first † to second † *as many* times
as specified.

( ) or [ ] — work enclosed instructions
as many times as specified by the
number immediately following *or* work
all enclosed instructions in the stitch or
space indicated *or* contains
explanatory remarks.

GAUGE: 16 dc and 8 rows = 2"

DRESS
Bodice
Leaving an 18" length at beginning for
Neck Edging, ch 14 *loosely;* being careful
not to twist ch, join with slip st to
form a ring.

Rnd 1 (Right side): Ch 3 *(counts as first dc, now and throughout)*, dc in same st, 2 dc in next ch, † ch 1, (dc, ch 1) 3 times in next ch, (dc, ch 1) twice in next ch, (dc, ch 1) 3 times in next ch †, 2 dc in each of next 4 chs, repeat from † to † once, 2 dc in each of last 2 chs; join with slip st to first dc: 32 dc.
Note: Loop a short piece of thread around any stitch to mark last round as *right* side.
Rnd 2: Ch 3, dc in next 3 dc, ch 1, skip next 9 ch-1 sps (Armhole), dc in next 8 dc, ch 1, skip next 9 ch-1 sps (Armhole), dc in last 4 dc; join with slip st to first dc: 16 dc.

Skirt
Rnd 1: Ch 6, working in each dc and in each ch around, dc in same st, ch 3, dc in next dc, ★ (ch 3, dc) twice in next st, ch 3, dc in next st; repeat from ★ around, ch 1, hdc in third ch of beginning ch-6 to form last ch-3 sp: 27 ch-3 sps.
Rnd 2: Ch 1, sc in same sp, (ch 3, sc in next ch-3 sp) around, ch 1, hdc in first sc to form last ch-3 sp.
Rnd 3: Ch 1, sc in same sp, 5 dc in next ch-3 sp, sc in next ch-3 sp, ★ ch 3, sc in next ch-3 sp, 5 dc in next ch-3 sp, sc in next ch-3 sp; repeat from ★ around, ch 1, hdc in first sc to form last ch-3 sp: 9 ch-3 sps.
Rnd 4: Ch 1, sc in same sp, (ch 3, skip next dc, sc in next dc) twice, ★ ch 3, sc in next ch-3 sp, (ch 3, skip next dc, sc in next dc) twice; repeat from ★ around, ch 1, hdc in first sc to form last ch-3 sp: 27 ch-3 sps.
Rnd 5: Ch 1, sc in same sp, ch 3, sc in next ch-3 sp, 5 dc in next ch-3 sp, ★ sc in next ch-3 sp, ch 3, sc in next ch-3 sp, 5 dc in next ch-3 sp; repeat from ★ around;

join with slip st to first sc: 9 ch-3 sps.
Rnd 6: Slip st in next ch-3 sp, ch 1, sc in same sp, (ch 3, skip next dc, sc in next dc) twice, ★ ch 3, sc in next ch-3 sp, (ch 3, skip next dc, sc in next dc) twice; repeat from ★ around, ch 1, hdc in first sc to form last ch-3 sp: 27 ch-3 sps.
Rnds 7-11: Repeat Rnds 5 and 6 twice, then repeat Rnd 5 once *more*.
Finish off.

Wing
Note: When instructed to join with sc, begin with a slip knot on hook. Insert hook in st indicated, YO and pull up a loop, YO and draw through both loops on hook.

Rnd 1: With *right* side facing and working in free loop of ch-1 (Fig. 1) *and* in skipped ch-1 sps of Armhole, join thread with sc in ch-1 at underarm; ch 3, sc around post of next dc, ch 3, (sc in next ch-1 sp, ch 3) 9 times, sc around post of next dc, ch 1, hdc in first sc to form last ch-3 sp: 12 ch-3 sps.

Fig. 1

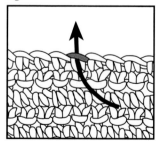

Rnd 2: Ch 1, sc in same sp, 5 dc in next ch-3 sp, sc in next ch-3 sp, ★ ch 3, sc in next ch-3 sp, 5 dc in next ch-3 sp, sc in next ch-3 sp; repeat from ★ around, ch 1, hdc in first sc to form last ch-3 sp: 4 ch-3 sps.

CHETED CLOTHESPIN
ELS (Continued)

: Ch 1, sc in same sp, (ch 3, skip
lc, sc in next dc) twice, ★ ch 3, sc
t ch-3 sp, (ch 3, skip next dc, sc in
lc) twice; repeat from ★ around,
hdc in first sc to form last ch-3 sp:
-3 sps.

: Ch 1, sc in same sp, ch 3, sc in
ch-3 sp, 5 dc in next ch-3 sp, ★ sc in
ch-3 sp, ch 3, sc in next ch-3 sp, 5 dc
xt ch-3 sp; repeat from ★ around;
with slip st to first sc, finish off.
at for second Wing.

O

1 (Right side): Ch 2, 8 sc in second
rom hook; join with slip st to first sc.
2: Ch 1, sc in same st, (ch 3, sc in
t sc) around, ch 1, hdc in first sc to
m last ch-3 sp: 8 ch-3 sps.
3: Ch 1, sc in same sp, ch 4, (sc in
t ch-3 sp, ch 4) around; join with
st to first sc, finish off.

ISHING
ck Edging
th right side facing and working in free
ps of beginning ch, insert hook in same
as joining, using beginning length, YO
d pull up a loop; ch 1, (slip st in next
, ch 1) around; join with slip st to first
p st, finish off.

ace Dress over clothespin. Glue Dress
d Halo to clothespin. Tie ribbon into a
w; trim ends. Glue bow to angel. For
nger, thread nylon thread through top
Halo and knot ends together.

CROCHETED SNOWFLAKES

Finished Size: approx. 2" dia.

MATERIALS
Bedspread Weight Cotton Thread
   (size 10), approx. 2 - 6 yards for
   each snowflake
Steel crochet hook, size 7 (1.65 mm)
Finishing supplies: Fabric stiffener, tracing
   paper, blocking or ironing board,
   plastic wrap, resealable plastic bag,
   rust-proof pins, terry towel, waterproof
   marking pen, and clear nylon thread
   for hanger

ABBREVIATIONS (see Crocheted
   Clothespin Angels instructions, page 72)

SNOWFLAKE 1
(top right snowflake in photo)
Ch 6; join with slip st to form a ring.
Rnd 1 (Right side): Ch 1, (sc in ring,
ch 5) 6 times; join with slip st to first sc:
6 ch-5 sps.
Rnd 2: Slip st in next ch-5 sp, ch 1, in
same sp and in each ch-5 sp around work
[3 sc, ch 5, slip st in third ch from hook,
(ch 3, slip st in third ch from hook)
4 times, slip st in first 2 chs of previous
ch-5, 3 sc]; join with slip st to first sc,
finish off.
Follow Snowflake Finishing instructions.

SNOWFLAKE 2
(center snowflake in photo)
Ch 6; join with slip st to form a ring.
Rnd 1 (Right side): Ch 6 *(counts as first
dc plus ch 3)*, (dc in ring, ch 3) 5 times;
join with slip st to first dc: 6 ch-3 sps.
Rnd 2: Slip st in next ch-3 sp, ch 1, in
same sp and in each ch-3 sp around work
[sc, hdc, dc, (ch 5, slip st in third ch from
hook) 3 times, ch 2, dc, hdc, sc]; join
with slip st to first sc, finish off.
Follow Snowflake Finishing instructions.

SNOWFLAKE 3
(lower right snowflake in photo)
Ch 6; join with slip st to form a ring.
Rnd 1 (Right side): Ch 1, (sc in ring,
ch 5) 6 times; join with slip st to first sc:
6 ch-5 sps.
Rnd 2: Slip st in next ch-5 sp, ch 1, in
same sp and in each ch-5 sp around work
(sc, hdc, dc, ch 5, slip st in third ch from
hook, ch 5, slip st in fifth ch from hook,
ch 3, slip st in third ch from hook, ch 2,
dc, hdc, sc, ch 3, slip st in third ch from
hook); join with slip st to first sc,
finish off.
Follow Snowflake Finishing instructions.

SNOWFLAKE FINISHING
1. (*Note:* Follow all steps for each
snowflake.) Using a mild detergent and
warm water, wash crocheted snowflake;
rinse thoroughly. Roll snowflake in terry
towel, gently pressing out excess
moisture. Lay snowflake flat and allow to
dry completely.
2. Pour fabric stiffener into plastic bag;
place snowflake in bag. Seal bag, pressing
out air. Work stiffener into snowflake and
allow to soak for several hours.
3. Trace snowflake pattern onto tracing
paper. Leaving at least 1" around design,
cut out pattern. Place pattern on blocking
board and cover with plastic wrap.
4. Remove snowflake from stiffener;
squeeze snowflake gently and blot with
paper towels to remove excess stiffener.
Place snowflake right side up over
pattern. Arrange snowflake to fit pattern,
using pins to pin snowflake in place.
Allow to dry.
5. For hanger, thread a 6" length of nylon
thread through chain space of ornament;
knot ends together.

Vintage handkerchiefs (found at a flea market!) are folded and tied in place to form a holiday dress for this sweet angel. A porcelain doll head and hands and padded wings add to her heirloom look.

HANDKERCHIEF ANGEL

You will need a 3"h porcelain angel head with 1½" long hands and a pair of 3" long padded wings (available at craft stores), 1 white and 1 print handkerchief (we found ours at a flea market), white fabric paint, gold glitter paint, small flat paintbrushes, 20" of ⅝"w wired satin ribbon, ⅔ yd of ⅛"w satin ribbon, 4" of ¹⁄₁₆" dia. gold cord, 2 miniature Christmas ornaments (we used a star and a glass ball), 6" of twisted paper, 16" of gold wired star garland, craft stick, and a hot glue gun and glue sticks.

1. (*Note:* Refer to Fig. 1 for Step 1.) For body of angel, glue 1 end of twisted paper into each hand for arms. Fold arms in half; glue center of arms into bottom of head. Glue 1 end of craft stick into bottom of head.

Fig. 1

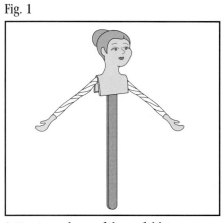

2. For inner layer of dress, fold 1 corner of white handkerchief 1½" to wrong side (Fig. 2). Gather folded edge of handkerchief around neck of angel; knot a 7" length of ⅛"w ribbon around handkerchief and neck (Fig. 3). Adjust gathers evenly and trim ribbon ends close to knot. Wrap adjacent corners of handkerchief around arms and glue to secure. Loosely fold side edges of handkerchief around craft stick and glue in place.

Fig. 2

Fig. 3

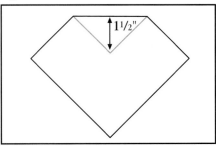

3. For outer layer of dress, wrap 2 adjacent corners of print handkerchief around neck to back of angel (Fig. 4); glue in place. Knot a 9" length of ⅛"w ribbon around waist of angel; trim ribbon ends close to knot. Adjust gathers and folds as desired; glue in place.

Fig. 4

4. Tie ⅝"w wired ribbon into an approx. 3"w bow; trim ends. Glue bow to waist of angel and arrange streamers.

5. Paint wings white; allow to dry. Brush wings and hair of angel with a light coat of gold glitter paint; allow to dry. Glue wings to back of angel.

6. Thread cord through hanger of 1 miniature ornament; knot ends together and glue to angel's hand. Repeat with remaining ⅛"w ribbon and remaining ornament.

7. For halo, form 1 end of star garland into a 1" dia. circle. With circle positioned over angel's head, glue garland to back of angel. Use "tail" of garland at back of angel to secure angel to tree.

PRESSED PANSY ORNAMENTS

*T*okens of your
affection, these pretty
tree-trimmers are easy
to craft using purchased
pressed pansies and glass
ball ornaments. Acrylic,
pearl, and glitter sprays
give the clear balls a
frosted finish.

PRESSED PANSY ORNAMENTS

For each ornament, you will need a
3" dia. clear glass ball ornament, 1 or
more pressed pansies (available at craft
stores), 10" of 1¹/₂"w organdy ribbon for
bow, 10" of ¹/₄"w satin ribbon for hanger,
spray adhesive, satin clear acrylic spray,
pearl craft spray, gold glitter craft spray,
craft glue (if needed), and a hot glue gun
and glue sticks.

1. Remove cap and hanger from
ornament.
2. (*Note:* Use a glass or cup with an
opening slightly smaller than ornament to
hold ornament while working.) Apply
spray adhesive to wrong side(s) of
flower(s) Working from center outward,
press flower(s) onto ornament as desired.
If necessary, use craft glue to secure edges
of flower(s) and allow to dry.
3. Allowing to dry after each coat, spray
ornament with acrylic spray, pearl spray,
and glitter spray.
4. Replace cap and hanger on ornament.
5. Tie organdy ribbon into a bow; trim
ends. Hot glue bow to top of ornament.
6. For hanger, thread satin ribbon through
hanger on ornament, knot ends together,
and trim ends.

ROMANTIC ENVELOPES

*B*rimming with *delicate flowers, our lacy miniature envelopes are true forget-me-nots for the holidays. The ornaments are easily fashioned from paper doilies and other sweet trims.*

ROMANTIC ENVELOPES

For each envelope, you will need heavy white paper, three 4" dia. white paper doilies, 11" of 1/16" dia. gold twisted cord, desired artificial flowers and leaves, desired gold charm (we used a heart and a key), tracing paper, and craft glue.

1. (*Note:* Allow to dry after each glue step.) Trace black lines of envelope back pattern, page 122, onto tracing paper; cut out. Use pattern to cut shape from white paper. Use a pencil to draw around 1 doily twice on a separate piece of white paper. Cut out circles approx. 1/4" inside drawn lines.
2. With doily extending just beyond top of envelope back paper piece, spot glue 1 doily to paper piece.
3. For envelope front, center and spot glue paper circles to backs of remaining doilies. Overlap edges of doilies approx. 1/2" and glue together at overlap.
4. To attach envelope front to envelope back, center envelope front on envelope back, referring to grey lines on envelope back pattern for placement of top edges of doilies. Fold edges of envelope front to back of envelope back and glue in place.

5. Arrange leaves and flowers in envelope as desired; glue in place. Glue charm to flowers or front of envelope.

6. For hanger, knot each end of cord; fray ends. Glue 1 knot to each side of envelope.

VICTORIAN TREASURES

These dainty trims are sure to be treasured. Little papier-mâché boxes are covered with wrapping paper and feminine frills to resemble Victorian hatboxes. For a romantic touch, a bouquet of small dried flowers is tucked inside a cone made from a gilded paper doily.

DECOUPAGED MINI HATBOXES

For each box, you will need a 3¹/₂" dia. papier-mâché box with lid, wrapping paper with desired motif, metallic gold acrylic paint, small flat paintbrushes, small foam brush, decoupage glue (either use purchased glue or mix 1 part craft glue with 1 part water to make glue), 9" of ¹/₁₆" dia. gold twisted cord, paper towels, hammer and awl, desired finish brush-on or spray sealer, and a low-temperature hot glue gun and glue sticks.

For music-motif box, you will *also* need 1"w gold loop fringe, ¹/₂" dia. and ⁵/₁₆" dia. gold ribbon roses, whitewash acrylic paint, and a small sponge piece.

For floral-motif box, you will *also* need 12" of ¹/₂"w gold ribbon.

MUSIC-MOTIF BOX

1. Remove lid from box. Use paintbrush to paint side of lid and bottom of box gold.
2. To decoupage box, measure around box; add 1". Measure height of box. Cut a strip of wrapping paper the determined measurements. Draw around top of lid on wrong side of paper; cut out circle.
3. Use foam brush to apply a thin coat of decoupage glue to sides of box.

Overlapping short edges, apply paper strip to sides of box; smooth in place and allow to dry (small wrinkles will disappear as glue dries). Repeat to apply paper circle to top of lid.

4. To sponge-paint box, dip dampened sponge piece in metallic gold paint; do not saturate. Remove excess paint on a paper towel. Using a light stamping motion, use sponge piece to paint box as desired; allow to dry.
5. Apply a coat of sealer to outside of box and lid; allow to dry.
6. (*Note:* Use hot glue for remaining steps.) For trim on box, cut a 12" length of loop fringe; glue fringe to side of lid. For decoration on top of lid, cut a length of loop fringe with 3¹/₂ loops (Fig. 1). Beginning with left end, gather bottom edge of 3 loops of fringe between fingers, forming a shamrock shape (Fig. 2); glue gathers together. Glue shamrock to center of lid.

Fig. 1

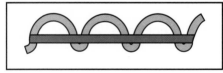

Fig. 2

7. Use a clean paintbrush to lightly brush a coat of whitewash on roses; allow to dry. Glue ⁵/₁₆" dia. roses to fringe on side of box lid as desired. Glue ¹/₂" dia. roses to center of shamrock.
8. For hanger, use hammer and awl to make 2 holes large enough for cord to pass through in opposite sides of box and in top of lid (Fig. 3). Thread ends of cord

through top of lid and out through sides of box; knot ends. Trim ends close to knots. Dot knots with glue to secure.

Fig. 3

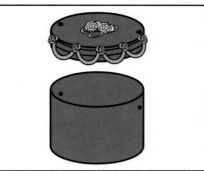

FLORAL-MOTIF BOX

1. Follow Steps 1, 2, 3, and 5 of Music-Motif Box instructions.
2. (*Note:* Use hot glue for remaining steps.) For trim on box, center and glue ribbon to side of lid, overlapping ends at back.
3. For hanger, follow Step 8 of Music-Motif Box instructions.

DAINTY BOUQUET ORNAMENT

You will need a 4" dia. gold paper doily, white paper, small dried flowers, 10" each of ¹/₄"w satin ribbon and ³/₁₆"w gold flat trim for hanger, and a hot glue gun and glue sticks.

1. Use a pencil to draw around doily on paper. Cut circle from paper ¹/₄" inside drawn lines.
2. Spot glue paper circle to center back of doily.
3. With right side of doily facing out and overlapping edges approx. ¹/₂", roll doily into a cone shape and glue edges together.
4. Arrange flowers in cone; glue to secure.
5. For hanger, knot ends of ribbon and trim together. Glue 1 knot to each side of cone.

GENTEEL PAPER DOLL

Dressed in a ruffled frock made of twisted paper and adorned with lace and ribbons, our old-fashioned paper doll ornament will add romance to the tree. Her genteel face is cut from a Victorian-style paper scrap.

VICTORIAN PAPER DOLL

For an approx. 10¹/₄"h doll, you will need an approx. 3¹/₂"h head and upper body paper cutout and a 2" long arm paper cutout, 12"w twisted paper for dress (untwisted), ³/₄"w lace for edging, ⁷/₈"w picot edge ribbon for sash, 24" of 1¹/₂"w organdy ribbon for bows, 6" of floral wire for hanger, poster board, tracing paper, and a hot glue gun and glue sticks.

1. For body of ornament, place head and upper body cutout under tracing paper. Beginning at shoulders, draw desired bodice and skirt shape onto tracing paper; cut out. Use pattern to cut shape from poster board. Glue head and upper body cutout to poster board.
2. For skirt and overskirt, measure length of skirt on poster board shape and multiply by 2. Cut a piece of twisted paper the determined length. Matching ends, fold twisted paper in half. Gather folded edge of twisted paper and glue along waist of skirt shape on ornament. Trim bottom edge of top layer of twisted paper (overskirt) to approx. 1" shorter than bottom layer of twisted paper (skirt).
3. For bodice and sleeves, cut a piece of twisted paper approx. 1" longer and 2" wider than bodice of ornament. Fold top

edge of paper ¹/₂" to 1 side (back) and make 1" long slits in bottom edge of paper piece approx. 1" from each side edge for sleeves (Fig. 1). With folded edge following contours of shoulders and arms of ornament, glue folded edge of paper piece to ornament. Trim bottom edge of bodice portion of paper piece even with waist of ornament. Gathering edge of paper piece as necessary, glue edge along waist of ornament.

Fig. 1

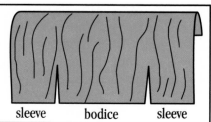

4. For sash, glue ribbon around waist of ornament, covering edges of bodice and skirt.
5. Gather and glue bottom edge of 1 sleeve to back of ornament. Gather and trim remaining sleeve as desired. Glue top of arm cutout to back of sleeve; glue arm cutout to dress to secure.
6. Glue lengths of lace trim along edges of sleeve and neckline. With lace extending approx. ¹/₄" beyond edges, glue lace trim to wrong side along bottom edges of dress.
7. For each bow on overskirt, tie an 8" length of organdy ribbon into a bow; trim ends. Glue bows to overskirt.
8. For hanger, bend wire length in half. Glue ends to top back of ornament.

FLEA MARKET BAUBLES

*B*ejeweled with faux
pearls, rhinestones, charms,
and more, these glittering
ornaments are fit for a
queen's evergreen! But you
don't have to be royalty to
enjoy the Yuletide baubles.
Inexpensive costume jewelry
found at flea markets
transforms painted wooden
cutouts into sparkling
pretties, especially when
finished with ornate
trims and bows.

FLEA MARKET JEWELRY ORNAMENTS

For each ornament, you will need a
2¹/₂" dia. wooden ornament-shaped
cutout, metallic gold spray paint, costume
jewelry pieces (we found our earrings,
necklaces, pins, and charms at a flea
market), desired trims to decorate
ornaments (we used gold cord, wired
ribbon, gold string pearls, and string
half-pearls), 4" of floral wire, wire cutters,
and a hot glue gun and glue sticks.

1. Spray paint wooden cutout gold; allow
to dry.
2. If necessary, remove backs from jewelry
pieces. Glue jewelry pieces to cutout as
desired, using wire cutters to cut to fit as
necessary.
3. Glue desired trim along edges of
ornament.

4. Tie ribbon or cord into a bow; trim
ends. Glue bow to top of ornament (For
cord bow, knot ends of bow streamers
together at base of ornament and glue
streamers to back of ornament to secure,
then glue a separate loop of cord to top
of bow).
5. For hanger, form a loop from wire and
glue ends to back of ornament.

81

FAUX LACE STOCKING

Steeped in old-fashioned beauty, these timeless ornaments take only a short time to make. A bow fashioned from iridescent wired ribbon and a coordinating cameo pendant are simply glued to a purchased tassel. To create the look of Battenberg lace on our miniature stocking, a pattern is traced onto the white cotton cuff, filled in with gold paint, and outlined with dimensional paint.

You will need two 6" x 9" pieces of gold fabric for stocking; two 6" x 9" fabric pieces for lining; one 4¹/₄" x 9" piece of white lightweight cotton fabric for cuff; thread to match fabrics; metallic gold fabric paint; iridescent white dimensional fabric paint in squeeze bottle with fine tip; small flat paintbrush; 7" of ¹/₈" dia. twisted cord for hanger; tracing paper; fabric marking pencil; and small, sharp scissors.

1. Trace stocking pattern onto tracing paper; cut out.
2. Use stocking pattern and follow *Sewing Shapes*, page 126, to make stocking from gold fabric pieces, leaving top edge of stocking open and trimming top edge of stocking along drawn line; do not turn right side out. Repeat to make stocking lining from lining fabric pieces; turn lining right side out.
3. Matching wrong sides, insert stocking into stocking lining; pin raw edges together.
4. For cuff, place cuff fabric piece over pattern, page 123, matching center of 1 long edge of fabric piece to center bottom of pattern. Use a pencil to lightly trace black lines of pattern onto fabric piece, extending pattern to short edges of fabric piece.
5. Use paintbrush to paint shaded areas of design on cuff gold; allow to dry. Referring to black and grey lines on pattern, use iridescent white paint to paint lines on cuff; allow to dry. Use scissors to carefully cut out cuff just outside bottom paint line.

6. Matching right sides and short edges, fold cuff in half. Using a ¹/₂" seam allowance, sew short edges together to form a tube. Finger press seam allowance open; do not turn right side out.
7. Matching raw edges of cuff and stocking lining, slip cuff over stocking lining. Center cuff seam at center back of stocking lining (with wrong side of front of cuff facing up, toe of stocking lining should point to right); pin raw edges together.
8. For hanger, place ends of cord between cuff and stocking lining at each side of stocking and match ends of cord to raw edges of cuff and stocking lining; pin in place.
9. Using a ¹/₂" seam allowance, sew cuff and hanger to stocking. Turn stocking right side out and press (do not press cuff).

CAMEO BOW

You will need a 2"h oval cameo pendant, a 4" long tassel, 26" of 2³/₄"w wired ribbon for bow, 15" of ¹/₁₆"w satin ribbon for hanger, and a hot glue gun and glue sticks.

1. Tie wired ribbon into an approx. 7"w bow; trim ends. Glue pendant to center of bow. Glue top of tassel to bottom back of pendant.
2. For hanger, thread satin ribbon through hanger on pendant and tie ends into a bow; trim ends.

SEED BEAD BOUQUETS

*S*mall in size yet big on versatility, seed beads are used to craft petite poinsettias, dainty leaves, and mistletoe berries for these Yuletide pretties. The beaded blossoms can be fashioned into a ribbon-tied nosegay or placed in a lace-trimmed gilded basket.

BEAD FLOWER BOUQUET AND BASKET

You will need iridescent white, gold, iridescent red, red, and iridescent green seed beads (we used the following colors of Mill Hill Glass Seed Beads: #00479 White, #02011 Victorian Gold, #02013 Red Red, #00968 Red, and #00431 Jade); 34-gauge gold wire; wire cutters; floral tape; and a hot glue gun and glue sticks. *For bouquet,* you will *also* need 12" of 3/8"w gold ribbon and 8" each of 1/8"w red and green ribbon.

For basket, you will *also* need a 1¹/₂" dia. basket, 5¹/₂" of 7/8"w white lace, metallic gold spray paint, and a piece of floral foam to fit in bottom of basket.

1. (*Note:* Follow Steps 1 - 5 to make 5 large flowers for bouquet or 4 large flowers for basket.) For large ring of petals, cut a 12" length of wire. Bend wire length in half. Thread 14 red or iridescent red beads onto center of wire; twist ends of wire together close to beads (Fig. 1). Thread 14 more beads onto 1 end of wire (Fig. 2). Twist wire to form a second petal. Repeat 1 more time on same wire end and 2 more times on remaining wire end. Arrange petals in flower shape and twist wire ends together to form stem.

Fig. 1   Fig. 2

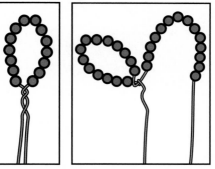

2. For small ring of petals, repeat Step 1, threading 10 beads onto wire for each petal and making 4 petals.
3. For flower center, cut a 4" length of wire. Bend wire length in half. Thread 4 gold beads onto center of wire. Twist ends of wire together close to beads.
4. For leaves, cut a 5" length of wire. Bend wire length in half. Thread 20 iridescent green beads onto center of wire. Twist ends of wire together close to beads. Thread 9 more beads onto 1 end of wire. Fold end of wire up so wire crosses center top of loop of beads (Fig. 3); fold end of wire to back of leaf. Twist wire ends together. Repeat to make a second leaf.

Fig. 3

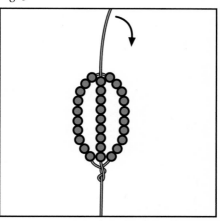

5. To assemble flower, place flower center at center of small ring of petals and small ring of petals at center of large ring of petals; twist wires together. Position leaves on flower stem as desired and twist leaf stems together with flower stem. Wrap stem with floral tape.
6. (*Note:* Follow Step 6 to make 8 berry clusters for bouquet or 3 berry clusters for basket.) Cut an 8" length of wire and follow Step 1, threading 5 iridescent white beads onto wire for each petal (set of berries) and making 3 petals. Wrap stem with floral tape.
7. For bouquet, trim stems of flowers and berry clusters to approx. 3". Twist stems of flowers and berry clusters together and wrap with floral tape. Beginning at bottom, wrap stems with gold ribbon; glue to secure. Tie red and green ribbon lengths into a bow around stems; trim ends.
8. For basket, spray paint basket gold; allow to dry. Glue lace trim along top edge of basket. Glue foam piece into basket. Trim stems of flowers and berry clusters to desired lengths and insert stems into foam as desired; glue to secure.

BEADED ICICLES

*T*hese romantic icicles are quick and easy to make by simply stringing pearls, buttons, beads, and golden accents together on metallic thread. Finished with dainty pink organdy bows, the feminine trims will shimmer in the tree's twinkling lights.

BEADED ICICLES

For each icicle, you will need assorted beads and buttons, heavy gold thread (we used Kreinik Balger® Fine #8 braid), two 9" lengths of ³/₄"w organdy ribbon, 2³/₄" long gold bolo tip for top of icicle, and a hot glue gun and glue sticks.

1. Thread a 1 yd length of thread onto a needle. Thread needle through point of bolo tip, leaving an approx. 5" tail of thread extending beyond point. Thread beads and buttons onto thread until icicle is approx. 8¹/₂" long, ending with a bead (to thread buttons onto thread, pass needle through 1 button hole, through opposite button hole, and back through first button hole again).
2. Pass needle back up through all beads and buttons except bottom bead. Pass needle back up through bolo tip and knot ends of thread at point of bolo tip to secure. For hanger, knot ends of thread together approx. 2¹/₄" from bolo tip; trim ends close to knot.
3. Tie ribbon lengths together into a bow; trim ends. Glue bow to top of bolo tip.

TUSSIE-MUSSIE TREE TOPPER

*O*ur tussie-mussie tree topper is reminiscent of the love tokens that Victorian suitors often gave their sweethearts. Regal silk roses, evergreen sprigs, and holly are cradled in a lacy paper doily to create the bouquet. A lavish bow and streamers fashioned from gilded plaid ribbon enhance the sentimental look.

TUSSIE-MUSSIE TREE TOPPER

You will need silk roses, small flowers, pine sprigs, holly, and ivy; 3¹/₄ yds of 1³/₈"w wired ribbon; approx. 5¹/₂" dia. white paper doily; clear acetate; floral wire; floral tape; wire cutters; permanent felt-tip pen; and a hot glue gun and glue sticks.

1. Arrange flowers and greenery into a bouquet and wire stems together close to flowers; trim stems to approx. 2" from wire. Wrap stems with floral tape.
2. Use pen to trace outer edge of doily onto acetate; cutting approx. ¹/₄" inside drawn circle, cut out circle. Center and spot glue doily to acetate circle.
3. Measure width of bouquet stem close to flowers in bouquet. Carefully cut a hole at center of doily the determined measurement.
4. With doily right side up, place stem of bouquet through center of doily; glue to secure.
5. Use ribbon to form a multi-loop bow with 4 streamers, wiring at center to secure; trim ends of streamers. Glue bow to bouquet stem.

PICTURE-PERFECT EMBROIDERY

*S*titched on black velvet, these embroidered silk ribbon flowers are especially elegant! Seed beads and a heart-shaped charm embellish the lovely blooms, which are showcased in a small gilded frame. Topped with a wired-ribbon bow and a cameo, this ornament is picture perfect.

SILK RIBBON EMBROIDERY ORNAMENT

You will need an 8" square of black velvet; YLI 4mm silk ribbon, DMC embroidery floss, and seed beads (see key, page 89); thread to match beads; embroidery and beading needles; square gold frame with 2³/8" opening; 31" of 1"w wired ribbon; ³/8"w gold heart charm; ⁵/8"w cameo charm; tissue paper; lightweight cardboard pieces cut to fit frame for insert and backing; tweezers (if needed); and a hot glue gun and glue sticks.

1. Use a pencil to trace embroidery pattern, page 89, onto tissue paper; cut out pattern 1¹/2" outside design. Center pattern on right side of velvet; pin or baste in place.
2. (*Note:* Refer to Stitch Diagrams, this page and page 89, to work embroidery stitches, using 16" lengths of silk ribbon.) Thread 1 end of ribbon length through eye of embroidery needle; pierce same end of ribbon ¹/4" from end with point of needle. Pull gently on remaining ribbon end, locking ribbon into eye of needle. Working over pattern, follow key, page 89,

to work embroidery design on velvet. Use beading needle and matching thread to sew on beads. Use blue ribbon to sew heart charm to design at "X."
3. Using tweezers if necessary, carefully tear pattern away from stitched design.
4. Center 1 cardboard piece (insert) on wrong side of stitched piece. Glue edges of stitched piece to back of insert.
5. Place insert and remaining cardboard piece (backing) in frame and secure in frame.
6. Cut a 13" length of wired ribbon; tie into an approx. 3"w bow and trim ends. Glue bow to center top of frame. Glue cameo to bow.
7. For hanger, fold remaining wired ribbon length in half. With approx. 2¹/2" of folded end of ribbon extending beyond top

of frame to form a loop, glue ribbon to frame back with streamers extending below frame. Trim ends as desired.

STITCH DIAGRAMS

Japanese Ribbon Stitch: Come up at 1. Lay ribbon flat on fabric and go down at 2, piercing ribbon (Fig. 1). Gently pull needle through to back; do not pull ribbon too tightly. Ribbon will curl at end of stitch as shown in Fig. 2.

Fig. 1

Fig. 2

Feather Stitch: Bring needle up at 1; keeping ribbon below point of needle, go down at 2 and come up at 3 (Fig. 3). Go down at 4 and come up at 5 (Fig. 4).

Fig. 3   Fig. 4

Wrapped Straight Stitch: Make a Straight Stitch (length of Straight Stitch determines size of petal). Come up at 1 (Fig. 5). Keeping ribbon flat, wrap ribbon around stitch without catching fabric or Straight Stitch with needle. Continue to wrap ribbon around Straight Stitch as desired. To end stitch, go down at 2 (Fig. 6).

Fig. 5   Fig. 6

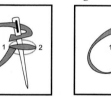

French Knot: Come up at 1. Wrap ribbon around needle and insert needle at 2, holding end of ribbon with non-stitching fingers (Fig. 7). Tighten knot, then pull needle through fabric, holding ribbon until it must be released.

Fig. 7

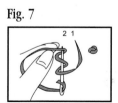

Spiderweb Rose: For anchor stitches, use 1 strand of floss to work 5 straight stitches from edge of circle to center, coming up at odd numbers and going down at even numbers (Fig. 8). For ribbon petals, bring needle up at center of anchor stitches; weave ribbon over and under anchor stitches (Fig. 9), keeping ribbon loose and allowing ribbon to twist. Continue to

weave ribbon until anchor stitches are covered.

Fig. 8   Fig. 9

Loop Stitch: Come up at 1. Use a large, blunt needle or toothpick to hold ribbon flat on fabric. Go down at 2, using blunt needle to hold ribbon flat while pulling ribbon through to back of fabric (Fig. 10). Leave blunt needle in loop until needle is brought up at 3 for next loop (Fig. 11). Continue working in this manner, forming desired number of loops.

Fig. 10   Fig. 11

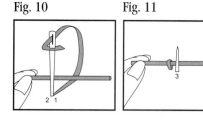

EMBROIDERY PATTERN

STITCH NAME	SYMBOL	YLI	DMC	MILL HILL BEADS
Japanese Ribbon Stitch		21	—	—
		170	—	—
Feather Stitch		170	—	—
Wrapped Straight Stitch		179	—	—
French Knot		46	—	—
Spiderweb Rose		112	760	—
		114	816	—
		156	ecru	—
Loop Stitch		51	—	—
Beads	●	—	—	62012
	●	—	—	62031

JUST FOR FUN

Christmas doesn't have to be just mistletoe and holly! With our bright Yuletide ideas, you can craft whimsical ornaments with their own unique style. From the personalized booties commemorating baby's first Christmas to handcrafted fish for your favorite angler, you'll find tree-trimmers for all the special people in your life. There are even adornments for folks who dream of spending their holidays in the sunny tropics. The beach ball, sand pail, and thong sandal ornaments shown here bring to mind an exhilarating day at the beach. You'll want to make every one of the clever cuties in this collection — just for the fun of it!

BEACH PARTY ORNAMENTS

BEACH BALL ORNAMENTS

For each ornament, you will need a 2¹/₂" dia. papier-mâché ball ornament, 6 colors of acrylic paint (we used white, yellow, orange, red, blue, and green), small flat paintbrushes, glossy clear acrylic spray, 4" of floral wire, 3 narrow rubber bands, and a hot glue gun and glue sticks.

1. (*Note:* Use a glass or cup with an opening slightly smaller than ornament to hold ornament while working.) For hanger, remove existing hanger from ornament. Glue 1 end of wire into top of ornament. Bend remaining end into a hook shape.

2. Overlapping rubber bands at top and bottom of ornament, place rubber bands around ornament, dividing ornament into 6 equal sections. Use a pencil to lightly draw along right side of each rubber band to mark ornament. Remove rubber bands. Connect lines at top and bottom of ornament.
3. Paint each section of ornament a different color; allow to dry.
4. Allowing to dry after each coat, apply 2 to 3 coats of acrylic spray to ball.

MINI SAND PAILS

For each pail, you will need a 2⁷/₈"h plastic cup for pail; 7" of ¹/₈" dia. paper wire for pail handle; 3" of ¹/₈" wooden dowel for shovel handle; a 3" square of aluminum flashing for shovel scoop; desired colors of acrylic spray paint for pail, pail handle, and shovel handle; floral foam to fill cup to ¹/₂" from rim; a 3" square of sandpaper; utility scissors; pliers; ¹/₄" hole punch; tracing paper; and a hot glue gun and glue sticks.

1. For pail, use hole punch to punch holes in opposite sides of cup near rim.
2. Spray paint pail, paper wire, and dowel desired colors; allow to dry.
3. For sand in pail, glue floral foam into pail. Draw around top of pail on back of sandpaper; use utility scissors to cut out circle just inside drawn lines. Place sandpaper circle over foam in pail, trimming to fit if necessary; glue in place.

4. For pail handle, place 1 end of paper wire into each hole in pail and bend ends up to secure.
5. For scoop of shovel, trace pattern onto tracing paper; cut out. Use pattern and utility scissors to cut scoop from flashing. Referring to red lines on pattern, make clips in scoop. Referring to blue lines on pattern, use pliers to fold up flaps A, B, and C. Referring to green line on pattern, use pliers to fold down flap D and wrap tabs of flap D around 1 end of dowel. Use dots of hot glue to secure.
6. Glue shovel to side of pail.

```
        tab   D   tab
             C
    A              B

        SCOOP
```

MINI BEACH SANDALS

For each sandal, you will need 2 colors of ¹/₁₆" thick crafting foam, serrated-cut craft scissors, craft knife, medium grit sandpaper (if needed), tracing paper, and a hot glue gun and glue sticks.

1. Trace sandal pattern onto tracing paper; cut out. Use pattern to cut 2 sandal shapes from 1 color of foam and 1 sandal shape from remaining color of foam. Layer sandal shapes together with same color shapes on top and bottom; glue shapes together. If necessary, use sandpaper to smooth edges of sandal. Referring to pattern and cutting through all layers, use craft knife to cut 3 small slits in sandal.
2. For straps, use craft scissors to cut two ¹/₂" x 2¹/₄" strips of foam. Overlap straps as shown in Fig. 1 and glue straps together. Use a crochet hook or point of closed scissors to push ends of straps into slits in sandal; glue straps into slits to secure.

Fig. 1

3. For hanger, use craft scissors to cut 1 side and regular scissors to cut remaining side of a ¹/₈" x 3¹/₂" strip of foam. Form strip into a loop and glue ends to bottom of sandal at heel end.

PEPPERMINT LIGHT BULB

*T*ransform a burned-out light bulb into a cheery peppermint-striped tree-trimmer using this bright idea. Simply paint on a red stripe and add a hanger fashioned from silver star garland. You'll have a no-fuss ornament in minutes!

PEPPERMINT LIGHT BULB

You will need a white light bulb, red acrylic enamel paint, small flat paintbrush, and approx. ¹/₂ yd of silver wired star garland.

1. Beginning at center top of light bulb (bottom of ornament) and ending at base, paint an approx. ¹/₂"w red stripe around bulb; allow to dry.
2. For hanger, wrap center of garland tightly around base of bulb and twist to secure. Twist ends of garland together approx. 1" from ends to form a loop.

FLOWERPOT SCHOOL BELL

This clever little bell gets an A⁺ for creativity! A small clay flowerpot is painted with school motifs, and a bell clapper is made using jute and a wooden bead. An outstanding gift for a teacher, the adornment is sure to be cherished for years.

SCHOOL BELL

You will need a 2¹/₂"h clay flowerpot, black acrylic paint, foam brush, white dimensional paint, fabric for trim, one ¹/₂" dia. and one 1" dia. red wooden bead, 4" of jute twine, 8" of ¹/₂"w "ruler" ribbon for hanger, 1" long twig, small silk leaf, and a hot glue gun and glue sticks.

1. Use foam brush to paint flowerpot black; allow to dry. Use white paint to write and draw on pot.
2. For fabric trim, measure width of rim of pot and add 1"; measure around rim and add ¹/₂". Cut a fabric strip the determined measurements. Press long edges of strip ¹/₂" to wrong side. Overlapping ends at back, glue trim to rim of pot.
3. For clapper, glue 1 end of twine into 1 end of small bead. Knot remaining end of twine and glue to inside bottom of pot.
4. For apple hanger, fold ribbon in half and glue ends into 1 end (top) of large bead. Glue twig and stem of leaf into top of bead. Glue hanger to top of bell.

WILD WEST BANDANNA

Corral a Western-style Christmas with our bandanna-wrapped ornament! Tied with rope and embellished with a painted wooden "sheriff's badge" cutout, this tree-trimmer will be enjoyed by cowpokes of all ages.

WILD WEST BANDANNA BALL

You will need a red bandanna or bandanna fabric, a 4" dia. papier-mâché ball ornament, 14" of ¼" dia. rope, 7" of jute twine, 2³/₈"w wooden sheriff's star cutout, silver spray paint, black permanent felt-tip pen with fine point, pinking shears, and a hot glue gun and glue sticks.

1. Use pinking shears to cut a 13" square from bandanna.
2. Remove existing hanger from papier-mâché ornament. Knot ends of twine together; glue knot into opening at top of ornament.
3. Place bandanna square wrong side up. Place ornament at center and gather edges of fabric at top of ornament. Tie rope around gathered fabric.
4. For sheriff's star, spray star cutout with silver paint; allow to dry. Use black pen to draw a dot at center of each star point and dashed lines along edges of star to resemble stitches. Glue star to rope.

ROLLER SKATE STOCKING

ROLLER SKATE STOCKING

Youngsters will get a kick out of this miniature stocking — it's shaped like a roller skate! Fusible fleece and fabric cutouts are machine stitched to make this cute ornament, and the green ribbon laces are threaded through painted-on eyelets. Filled with candy canes or other treats, the skate will make a fun party favor, too!

You will need a 10" square of white fabric for skate, a 5" square of red fabric for heel and toe, a 7" square of black fabric for wheels, fusible fleece, paper-backed fusible web, four $7/8$" dia. white buttons, $5/8$ yd of $1/16$"w green satin ribbon for bootlace, $1/3$ yd of $1/16$"w red satin ribbon, 4" of $1/4$"w red satin ribbon for hanger, white thread, needle with large eye, pinking shears, red dimensional paint for eyelets, tracing paper, liquid fray preventative, fabric marking pencil, and a hot glue gun and glue sticks.

1. Follow manufacturer's instructions to fuse fleece to wrong sides of white and black fabrics. Follow manufacturer's instructions to fuse web to wrong side of red fabric.
2. Trace patterns onto tracing paper; cut out. Use patterns to cut indicated numbers of skate and wheel shapes from fabrics. Use patterns and pinking shears to cut indicated numbers of heel and toe shapes from fabric. Referring to skate pattern, use fabric marking pencil to mark dots for eyelets on each skate shape.
3. Remove paper backing from toes and heels and fuse to skate shapes.
4. Pin skate shapes fleece sides together. Using a $1/4$" seam allowance and leaving top edge open, sew skate shapes together. Trim seam allowance to $1/8$".
5. Pin 2 wheel shapes fleece sides together. Using a $1/4$" seam allowance, sew wheel shapes together. Trim seam allowance to $1/8$". Repeat to sew remaining wheel shapes together.
6. Apply fray preventative to raw edges of fabric shapes; allow to dry.
7. For eyelets in skate, use red paint to paint a small circle around each marked dot on 1 side of skate; allow to dry. Repeat for remaining side of skate.
8. For bootlace, thread needle with green ribbon. Beginning and ending at top eyelets on skate, lace ribbon through eyelets in skate. Tie ribbon ends into a bow at top of skate and trim ends.
9. For each set of wheels, glue 2 wheels together. Cut $1/16$"w red ribbon into four 3" lengths. Thread 1 ribbon length through holes in each button and knot ends at back; trim ends. Glue 1 button to each side of each wheel set.
10. Glue wheel sets to bottom edge of skate.
11. For hanger, fold $1/4$"w red ribbon in half and glue ends to top back edge of skate.

SKATE
(cut 2 from white fabric,
1 in reverse)

WHEEL
(cut 8 from black fabric)

HEEL
(cut 2 from
red fabric,
1 in reverse)

TOE
(cut 2 from red fabric,
1 in reverse)

"CANDY SEED" PACKETS

*D*ecorated with winsome hand-colored designs, our cute "seed packet" ornaments will delight all your holiday guests. You may even want to enclose some small buttons in the envelopes to make it sound like the packets are actually filled with seeds. Smiles are sure to blossom wherever these pretty packets are "planted!"

SEED PACKET ORNAMENTS

For each seed packet, you will need either red or green paper, red and green colored pencils, Design Master® glossy wood tone spray, assorted buttons, jumbo craft stick, utility scissors, tracing paper, rubber cement, and a hot glue gun and glue sticks.

1. Make a photocopy of desired seed packet design, page 124. Use colored pencils to color photocopy. Spray photocopy lightly with wood tone spray; allow to dry. Cut out design.
2. Use seed packet pattern, page 124, and follow *Tracing Patterns*, page 126. Use pattern to cut shape from red or green paper. Referring to grey lines on pattern, fold side flaps, then top and bottom flaps of paper piece to 1 side (wrong side). Use rubber cement to glue side and bottom flaps together to secure.

3. Use rubber cement to glue colored photocopy to front of seed packet.
4. Hot glue buttons to seed packet. If desired, place several buttons inside packet for "seeds."

5. Use utility scissors to cut a point at 1 end of craft stick. With pointed end of craft stick extending approx. 2" below seed packet, hot glue stick to center back of packet.

GLITZY "STAINED GLASS"

To create a stained glass look on these tree-trimmers, we glued pieces of colorful tissue paper to the outside of clear glass balls and sprinkled them with glitter. Stuffed with gold star garland, the ornaments will make a sparkling addition to the tree.

"STAINED GLASS" ORNAMENTS

For each ornament, you will need a 3" dia. clear glass ball ornament, gold wired star garland, wire cutters, gold glitter, assorted colors of tissue paper, decoupage glue (either use purchased glue or mix 1 part craft glue with 1 part water to make glue), and a foam brush.

1. Remove cap and hanger from ornament and fill ornament with garland as desired; replace cap and hanger on ornament.
2. Tear a small piece of tissue paper and place on ornament. Use foam brush to apply glue over paper piece, smoothing paper piece onto ball. Using varying sizes of paper pieces and leaving some areas of ornament uncovered, repeat to apply more paper pieces to ornament, overlapping pieces as desired. Before glue dries, sprinkle glitter on ornament; allow to dry and shake off excess glitter.
3. For garland hanger, wrap 1 end of a 6" length of garland tightly around cap of ornament and twist to secure. Pass remaining end of garland through hanger on ornament, wrap around finger to curl, and form a hook shape at end.

GARDEN GNOME

A protector of the earth's treasures, this little gnome spreads Yuletide cheer from his happy woodland home. He's displayed in a small clay flowerpot that's decorated with faux ivy, mushrooms, and bees.

GARDEN GNOME

You will need an approx. 3"h clay flowerpot, 2¹/₂"h porcelain Santa head (available at craft stores), craft stick, white wool doll hair, 5" of 2"w gold burlap ribbon, floral foam to fit in pot, sheet moss, approx. 16" of latex ivy, artificial pine sprig with miniature pinecones, artificial mushrooms, bee floral picks, miniature rake, and a hot glue gun and glue sticks.

1. Glue floral foam into pot. Glue moss over foam. Glue craft stick into bottom of Santa head.
2. For beard and hair on gnome, glue lengths of doll hair to face and head, arranging and trimming as desired.
3. For hat, place ribbon with long edges at top and bottom. Overlap top corners of ribbon to form a cone shape; glue corners together to secure. With overlap at back, glue hat to gnome. Glue pine sprig to 1 side of hat.
4. Insert gnome head, mushrooms, and bees into pot.
5. Glue ivy around pot, arranging as desired. Glue rake to pot.

KITCHEN POMANDERS

*C*overed with dried kidney beans, chives, crushed red pepper, split peas, and pumpkin seeds, papier-mâché balls become pomander-style ornaments to display all year long. We used strands of raffia for the hangers and aromatic bay leaves to accent the tops of these kitchen creations.

CHRISTMAS KITCHEN ORNAMENTS

For each ornament, you will need a 2¹/₂" dia. papier-mâché ball ornament; several 8" strands of dark red raffia; 2 bay leaves; desired dried peas, beans, seeds, or herbs (we used split peas, kidney beans, pumpkin seeds, crushed red pepper, and crushed chives); and a low-temperature hot glue gun and glue sticks.
For ornament covered with peas, beans, or seeds, you will *also* need green spray paint or Design Master® glossy wood tone spray (optional).
For ornament covered with crushed herb, you will *also* need a paper plate, craft glue, and a foam brush.

1. Remove existing hanger from ornament.
2. Before covering ornament with peas, beans, or seeds, place ornament on a protected surface and either spray paint it green or spray it lightly with wood tone spray if desired. Allow to dry.
3. (*Note:* Use a glass or cup with an opening slightly smaller than ornament to hold ornament while working.) Fold raffia strands in half and hot glue ends into top of ornament.
4. To cover ornament with peas, beans, or seeds, begin at top of ornament and hot glue a ring of peas, beans, or seeds around hanger. Glue peas, beans, or seeds to ornament until ornament is covered, overlapping seeds as desired.

5. To cover ornament with a crushed herb, spread a thick layer of herb on paper plate. Use foam brush to apply a thin layer of craft glue to ornament. Roll ornament in herb; allow to dry. Repeat as necessary until ornament is covered.
6. Cross bay leaves and hot glue together. Make a small hole at center of leaves and thread onto raffia hanger on ornament.

NIFTY BILLIARD BALLS

BILLIARD BALL ORNAMENTS

You don't have to be a billiards buff to enjoy these novelty ornaments. Papier-mâché balls are painted to resemble pool balls, and clear sealer gives them a realistic glossy shine. You'll rack up lots of compliments on these nifty tree-trimmers!

For each ball, you will need a 2½" dia. papier-mâché ball ornament, ivory and black acrylic paint, small flat and round paintbrushes, glossy clear acrylic spray, tracing paper, graphite transfer paper, and a drawing compass.

For solid ball, you will *also* need yellow, red, or green acrylic paint.

For striped ball, you will *also* need orange or purple acrylic paint, a 4" square of tagboard (manila folder), and a craft knife.

SOLID BALL

1. (*Note:* Use a glass or cup with an opening slightly smaller than ornament to hold ornament while working.) Paint ornament yellow, red, or green; allow to dry.

2. For number background, use compass to draw a 1" dia. circle on 1 side (front) of ornament. Paint circle ivory; allow to dry.

3. Trace number 3, 6, or 9 pattern onto tracing paper. Use transfer paper to transfer number to center of number background on ornament. Paint number black; allow to dry.

4. Allowing to dry after each coat, spray ornament with 2 to 3 coats of acrylic spray.

STRIPED BALL

1. Follow Step 1 to paint ornam[...]

2. For stripe t[...] pattern onto tracing p[...] around pattern at center of tagbo[...] craft knife to cut circle from tagboard; discard circle.

3. To draw top edge of stripe on ornament, center template on top of ornament and draw around ornament where tagboard touches ornament (Fig. 1); repeat to draw bottom edge of stripe on bottom of ornament.

Fig. 1

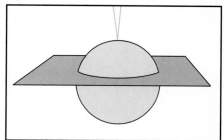

4. For number background, use compass to draw a 1" dia. circle at center of stripe on 1 side (front) of ornament.

5. Leaving number background unpainted, paint stripe orange or purple; allow to dry.

6. Follow Steps 3 and 4 of Solid Ball instructions to paint number 12 or 13 on ornament and seal ornament.

TEMPLATE

3 6 9 12 13

BREEZY SANTA

*his whimsical
nta windsock is a breeze
o make using crafting
foam and ribbons. The
colorful streamers add
festive flair to the
miniature merrymaker.*

MINI SANTA WINDSOCK

You will need white, peach, and red ¹/₁₆"
thick crafting foam; 30" each of red and
green ³/₈"w satin ribbon; 8" of green
¹/₁₆"w satin ribbon; black permanent felt-
tip pen with fine point; white acrylic paint;
small round paintbrush; tracing paper;
and a hot glue gun and glue sticks.

1. Trace patterns, page 123, onto tracing
paper; cut out. Use patterns to cut beard,
mustache, hat trim, and pom-pom from
white foam and hat and nose from red
foam. Cut a 2³/₈" x 4³/₄" rectangle from
peach foam for face.
2. For streamers, cut each ³/₈"w ribbon
length into five 6" lengths. Position peach
foam piece with long edges at top and
bottom. Place ribbon lengths right sides
down. Beginning at left end of bottom
edge of foam piece and alternating red
and green ribbon lengths, glue ¹/₂" at 1
end of each ribbon length at bottom of
foam piece. Trim ribbon ends.

3. For face, overlap short edges of foam
piece ¹/₂" with streamers to inside to form
a tube (overlap is back); glue to secure.
4. Glue hat trim and pom-pom to hat. Glue
mustache and nose to beard. Glue hat and
beard to face.

5. Use black pen to draw dots for eyes.
Use white paint to paint eyebrows; allow
to dry.
6. For hanger, glue 1 end of ¹/₁₆"w ribbon
into top of face at each side.

CHRISTMAS BOOTIES

F or a sweet way to remember baby's first Christmas, craft this quick-and-easy tree-trimmer! Satin baby shoes are personalized using a permanent marker and embellished with red ribbon laces and miniature ornaments. A polka dot wired-ribbon bow completes the keepsake ornament.

BABY'S FIRST CHRISTMAS ORNAMENT

You will need a pair of white satin baby shoes, 2 miniature Christmas ball ornaments, 1/4"w red satin ribbon for shoelaces, 10" of 1/4"w white satin ribbon for hanger, 20" of 2 1/2"w wired ribbon for bow, green (optional) and red permanent felt-tip pens with fine points, tissue paper, and a hot glue gun and glue sticks.

1. Remove laces from shoes. Stuff toe of each shoe with tissue paper.
2. Use red pen to write baby's name and birth date on toe of 1 shoe and "Baby's First Christmas" on toe of remaining shoe. If desired, use green pen to color over decorative stitching on shoes.
3. For shoelaces, cut 2 lengths of red ribbon same length as shoelaces. Lace shoes with ribbons, thread ornaments onto ribbons, and tie into bows; trim ends.
4. For hanger, fold white ribbon in half and knot 1 1/2" from fold to form a loop. Glue 1/2" at 1 end of ribbon to back of each shoe.
5. For bow, tie wired ribbon into a bow; trim ends. Glue bow to knot in hanger.

FISHY FAVORITES

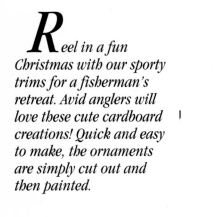

*R**eel in a fun Christmas with our sporty trims for a fisherman's retreat. Avid anglers will love these cute cardboard creations! Quick and easy to make, the ornaments are simply cut out and then painted.*

FISH ORNAMENTS AND "GONE FISHING" SIGN

You will need corrugated cardboard; white, red, green and other desired colors of acrylic paint (we used yellow, peach, rust, light green, dark green, tan, and dark grey); small flat and round paintbrushes; black permanent felt-tip pen with fine point; craft knife and cutting mat; and tracing paper.

1. Trace sign and desired fish patterns, page 125, onto tracing paper; cut out. Use patterns and craft knife to cut shapes from cardboard.
2. To paint sign, mix 1 part green paint with 3 parts water. Use flat paintbrush and paint mixture to paint sign; allow to dry. Use round paintbrush and red paint to paint "gone fishing" on sign; allow to dry.
3. To paint fish, use paintbrushes to paint and shade fish as desired (we blended the paint colors on 2 of our fish before the paint dried). Allowing to dry after each color, use tip of paintbrush handle to paint dots on body and white dots for eyes. Use black pen to color pupils in eyes and draw detail lines on fins.

SAFARI BALLS

*I*f you crave the exotic, then you'll love our African safari-inspired ornaments! Papier-mâché balls are painted with zebra, giraffe, and leopard markings for a "call of the wild" look. Raffia and bead hangers finish these unique adornments.

ANIMAL-PRINT ORNAMENTS

For each ornament, you will need a 4" dia. papier-mâché ball ornament; 17" of natural raffia; 2 wooden beads; the following colors of acrylic paint: white and black for zebra ornament, ivory and brown for giraffe ornament, or ivory, black, and dark yellow for leopard ornament; paintbrushes; matte clear acrylic spray; and a hot glue gun and glue sticks.

1. (*Note:* Use a glass or cup with an opening slightly smaller than ornament to hold ornament while working.) For hanger, remove existing hanger from ornament. Fold raffia length in half; glue fold of raffia into opening at top of ornament. Thread beads onto raffia. Knot ends of raffia together approx. 6" from ornament.

2. (*Note:* Allow to dry after each paint color.) For zebra ornament, paint ornament white; paint black irregular stripes on ornament. For giraffe ornament, paint ornament ivory; paint brown irregular spots on ornament. For leopard ornament, paint ornament ivory; use straight brush strokes to paint black irregular spots on ornament, then smaller dark yellow spots at centers of black spots.

3. Spray ornament with clear acrylic spray. Allow to dry.

107

PATTERNS

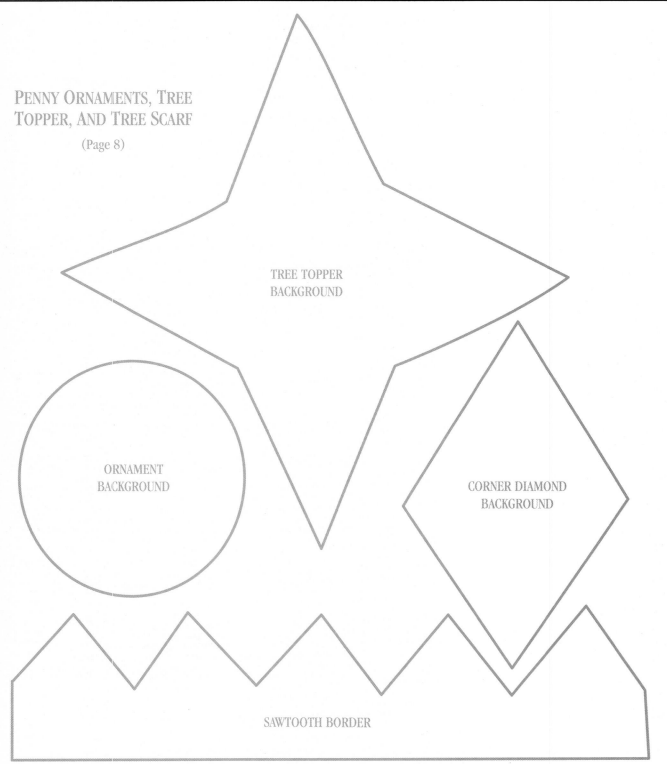

PENNY ORNAMENTS, TREE
TOPPER, AND TREE SCARF

(Page 8)

TREE TOPPER
BACKGROUND

ORNAMENT
BACKGROUND

CORNER DIAMOND
BACKGROUND

SAWTOOTH BORDER

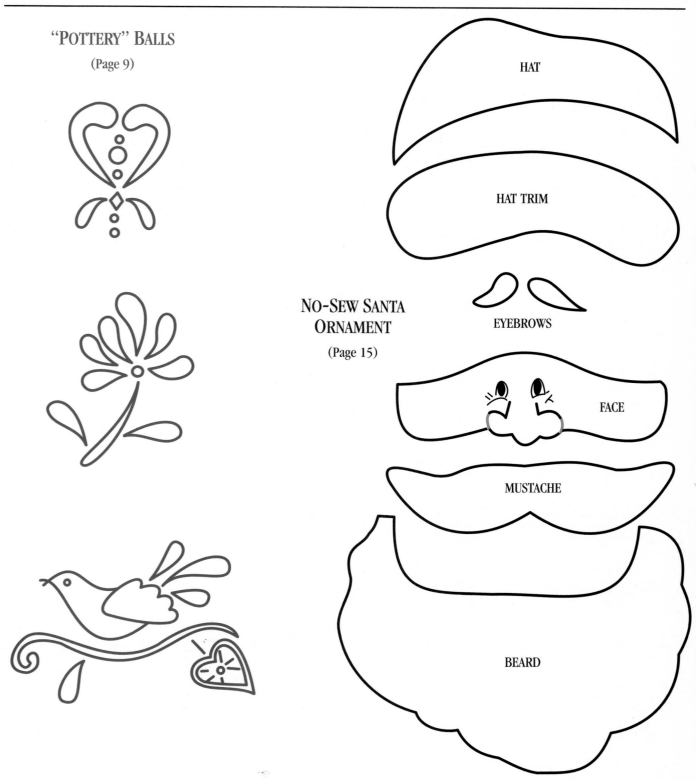

"POTTERY" BALLS

(Page 9)

NO-SEW SANTA
ORNAMENT

(Page 15)

HAT

HAT TRIM

EYEBROWS

FACE

MUSTACHE

BEARD

PATTERNS (continued)

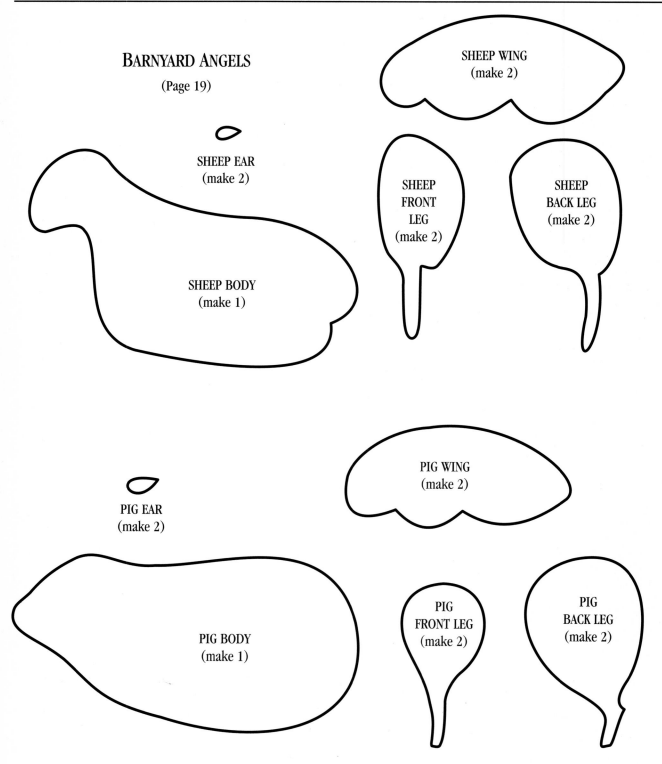

BARNYARD ANGELS

(Page 19)

SHEEP EAR
(make 2)

SHEEP WING
(make 2)

SHEEP
FRONT
LEG
(make 2)

SHEEP
BACK LEG
(make 2)

SHEEP BODY
(make 1)

PIG EAR
(make 2)

PIG WING
(make 2)

PIG BODY
(make 1)

PIG
FRONT LEG
(make 2)

PIG
BACK LEG
(make 2)

BARNYARD ANGELS

(Page 19)
(continued)

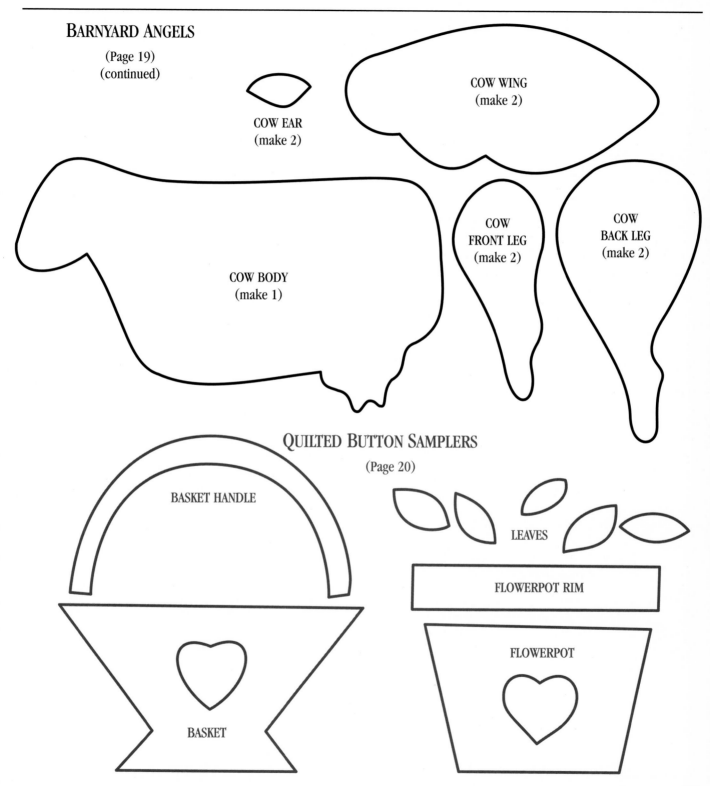

COW EAR
(make 2)

COW WING
(make 2)

COW BODY
(make 1)

COW
FRONT LEG
(make 2)

COW
BACK LEG
(make 2)

QUILTED BUTTON SAMPLERS

(Page 20)

BASKET HANDLE

LEAVES

FLOWERPOT RIM

FLOWERPOT

BASKET

PATTERNS (continued)

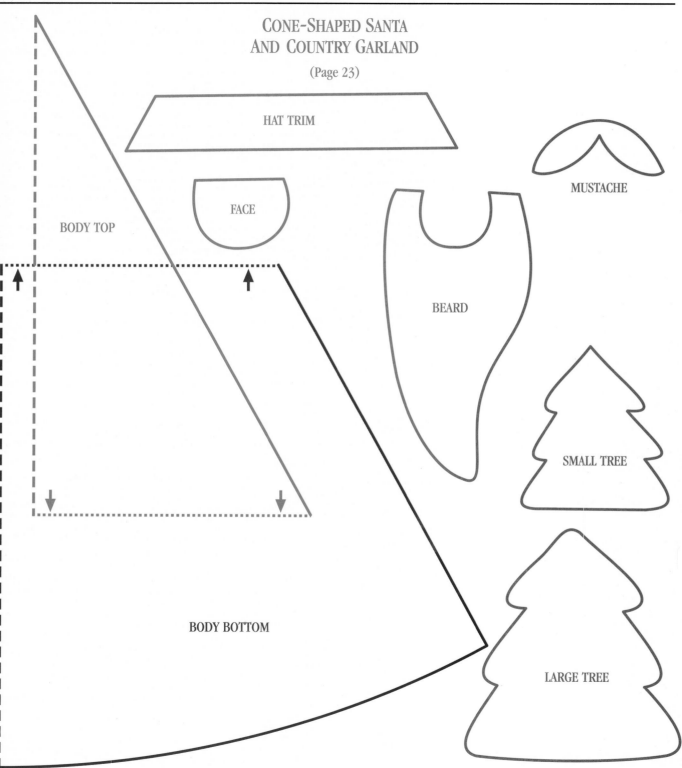

CONE-SHAPED SANTA
AND COUNTRY GARLAND

(Page 23)

HAT TRIM

MUSTACHE

FACE

BODY TOP

BEARD

BODY BOTTOM

SMALL TREE

LARGE TREE

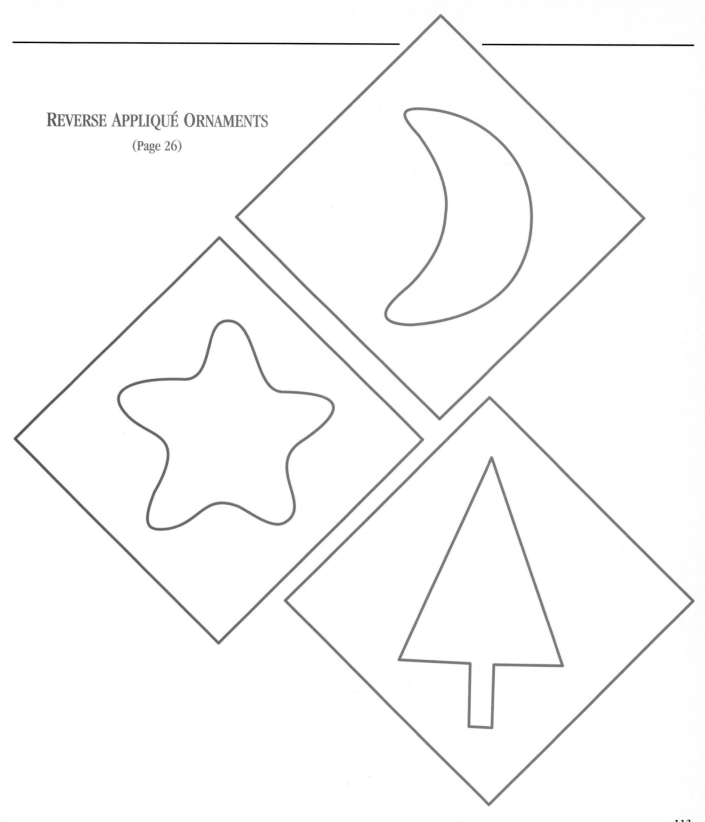

Reverse Appliqué Ornaments

(Page 26)

PATTERNS (continued)

PEEK-A-BOO SNOWMAN
(Page 27)

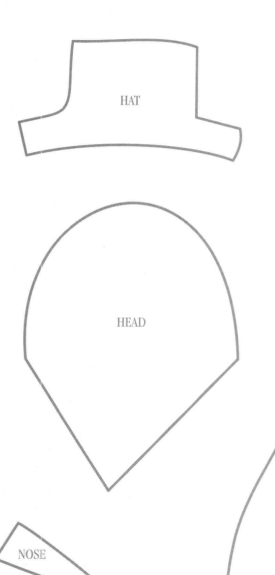

HAT

HEAD

NOSE

STOCKING

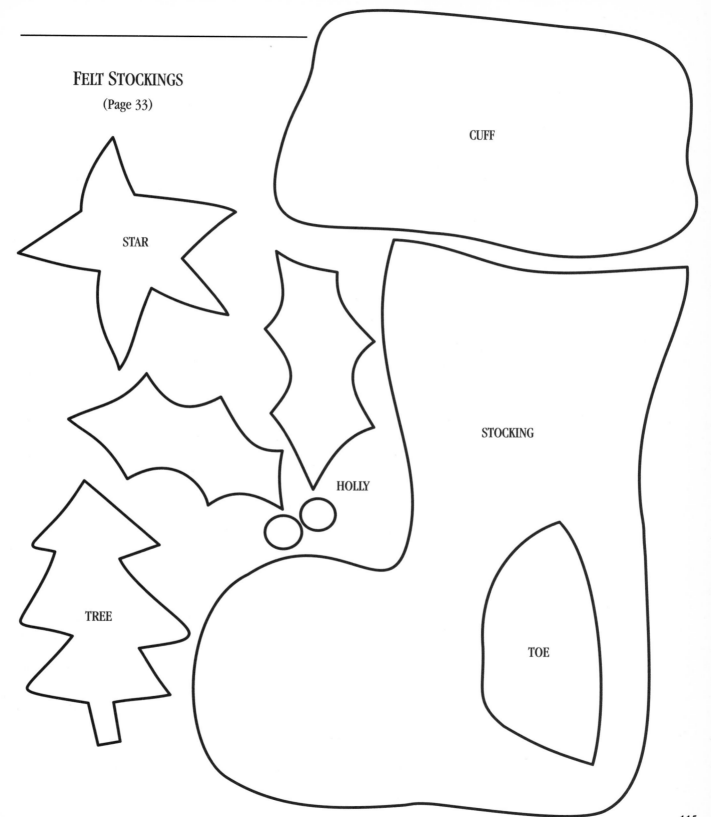

FELT STOCKINGS

(Page 33)

STAR

CUFF

HOLLY

STOCKING

TREE

TOE

PATTERNS (continued)

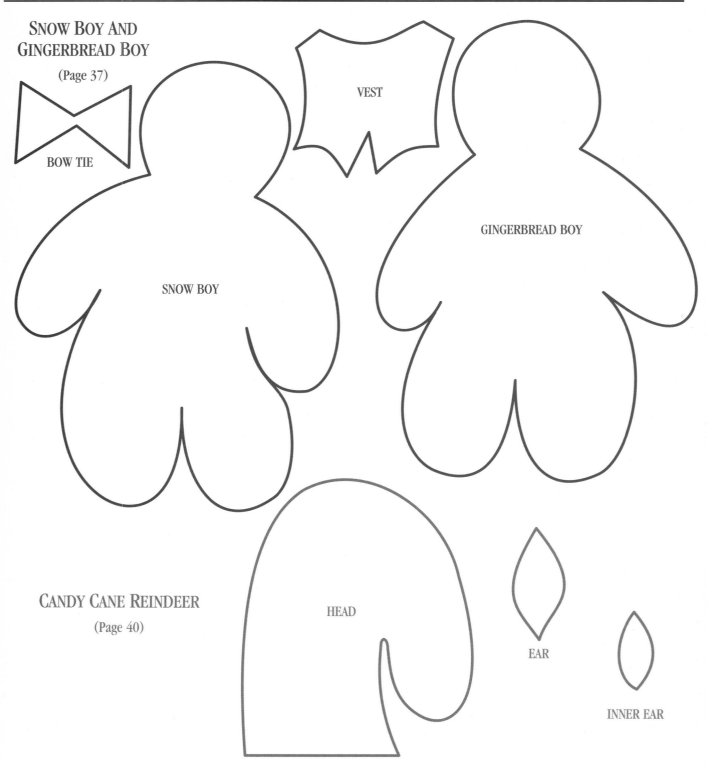

SNOW BOY AND
GINGERBREAD BOY

(Page 37)

BOW TIE

VEST

GINGERBREAD BOY

SNOW BOY

CANDY CANE REINDEER

(Page 40)

HEAD

EAR

INNER EAR

CHRISTMAS TREE FRAME

(Page 41)

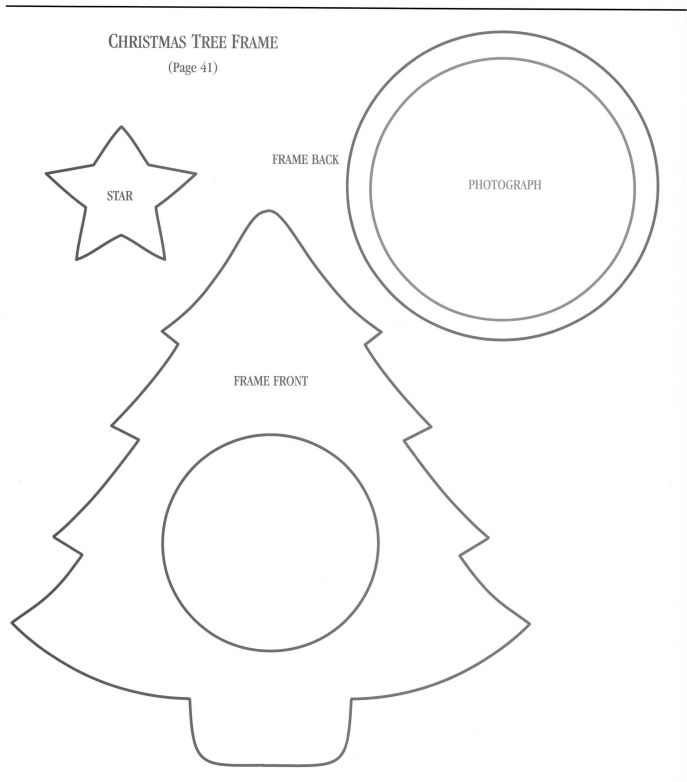

STAR

FRAME BACK

PHOTOGRAPH

FRAME FRONT

PATTERNS (continued)

HAT TRIM

PLAYFUL PENGUINS

(Page 47)

MERRY BEAD SANTA

(Page 43)

HAT

POM-POM

HAT

HAT TRIM

EYEBROWS

FACE

MUSTACHE

CHEST

CHEEK
(cut 2)

BEARD

BODY

BODY

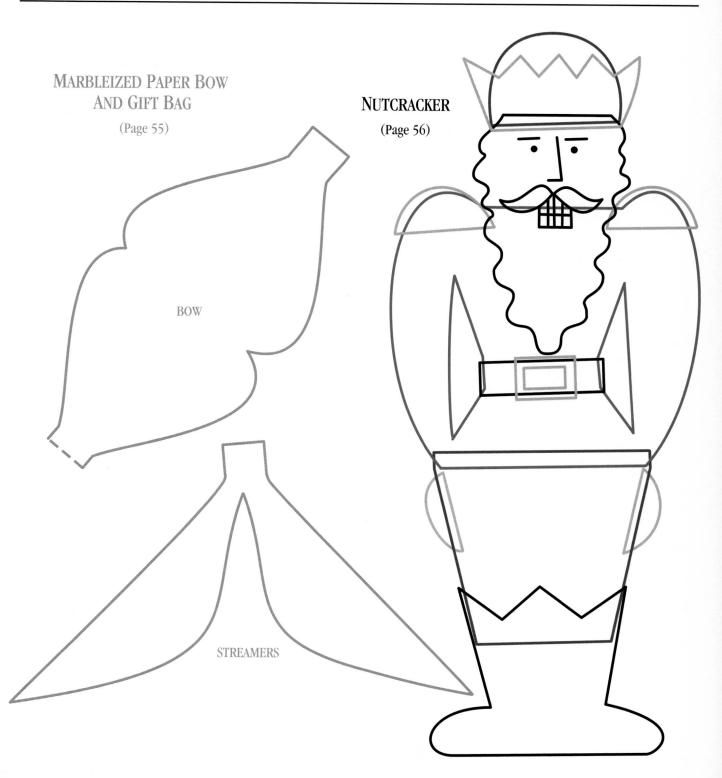

MARBLEIZED PAPER BOW
AND GIFT BAG

(Page 55)

NUTCRACKER

(Page 56)

BOW

STREAMERS

119

DIMENSIONAL SNOWFLAKES
(Page 57)

HEIRLOOM ANGEL ORNAMENTS

(Page 59)

The designs on this page are copyright-free and may be photocopied for personal use.

PATTERNS (continued)

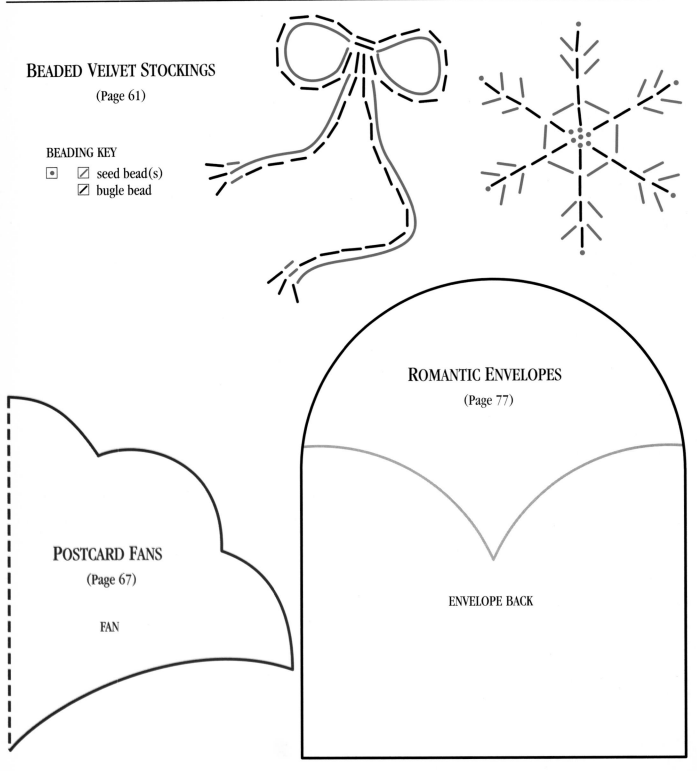

BEADED VELVET STOCKINGS

(Page 61)

BEADING KEY

- ⊡ ☑ seed bead(s)
- ☑ bugle bead

ROMANTIC ENVELOPES

(Page 77)

ENVELOPE BACK

POSTCARD FANS

(Page 67)

FAN

FAUX LACE STOCKING

(Page 83)

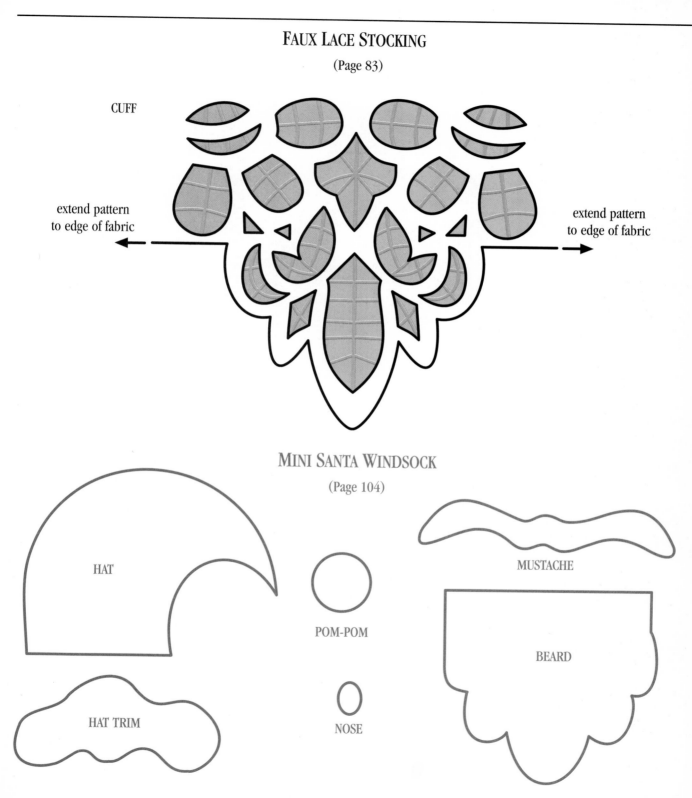

CUFF

extend pattern
to edge of fabric

extend pattern
to edge of fabric

MINI SANTA WINDSOCK

(Page 104)

HAT

HAT TRIM

POM-POM

NOSE

MUSTACHE

BEARD

PATTERNS (continued)

SEED PACKET ORNAMENTS

(Page 98)

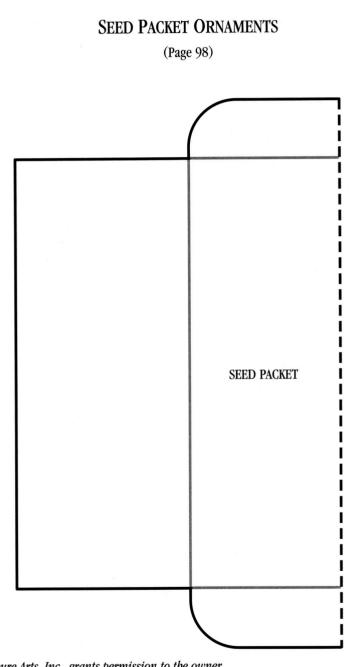

SEED PACKET

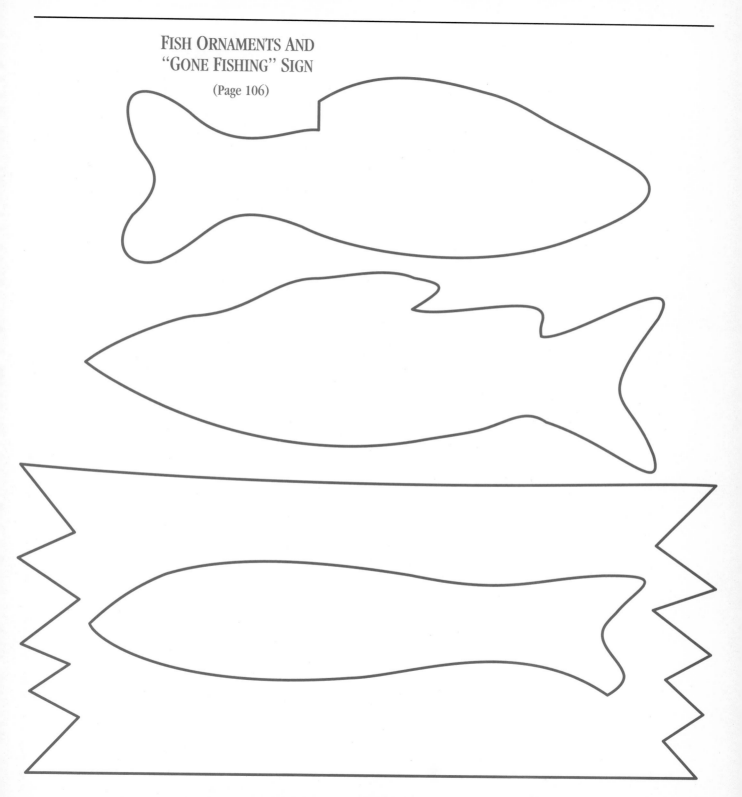

FISH ORNAMENTS AND
"GONE FISHING" SIGN

(Page 106)

GENERAL INSTRUCTIONS

TRACING PATTERNS

When entire pattern is shown, place tracing paper over pattern and trace pattern; cut out. For a more durable pattern, use a permanent pen to trace pattern onto acetate; cut out.

When only half of pattern is shown (indicated by dashed line on pattern), fold tracing paper in half and place fold along dashed line of pattern. Trace pattern half; turn folded paper over and draw over traced lines on remaining side of paper. Unfold pattern and lay pattern flat; cut out. For a more durable pattern, use a permanent pen to trace pattern half onto acetate; turn acetate over and trace pattern half again, aligning dashed lines to form a whole pattern; cut out.

SEWING SHAPES

1. Center pattern on wrong side of 1 fabric piece and use fabric marking pencil or pen to draw around pattern. DO NOT CUT OUT SHAPE.
2. Place fabric pieces right sides together. Leaving an opening for turning, carefully sew pieces together directly on pencil line.
3. Leaving a 1/4" seam allowance, cut out shape. Clip seam allowance at curves and corners. Turn shape right side out.

MAKING APPLIQUÉS

1. (*Note:* Follow all steps for each appliqué. When tracing patterns for more than 1 appliqué, leave at least 1" between shapes on fusible web. To make a reverse appliqué, trace pattern onto tracing paper, turn traced pattern over, and follow all steps using traced pattern.) Trace appliqué pattern onto paper side of web.
2. Cutting approx. 1/2" outside drawn lines, cut out web shape.
3. (*Note:* If using a thin fabric for appliqué over a dark or print fabric, follow manufacturer's instructions to fuse interfacing to wrong side of fabric before completing Step 3.) Follow manufacturer's instructions to fuse web shape to wrong side of fabric. Cut out shape along drawn lines.

CROSS STITCH

COUNTED CROSS STITCH (X)
Work 1 Cross Stitch to correspond to each colored square in chart. For horizontal rows, work stitches in 2 journeys (Fig. 1). For vertical rows, complete each stitch as shown in Fig. 2. When working over 2 fabric threads, work Cross Stitch as shown in Fig. 3. When chart shows a Backstitch crossing a colored square (Fig. 4), a Cross Stitch (Fig. 1, 2, or 3) should be worked first, then Backstitch (Fig. 6) should be worked on top of Cross Stitch.

Fig. 1

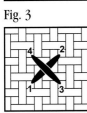

Fig. 2

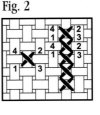

Fig. 3

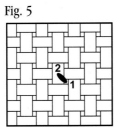

Fig. 4

QUARTER STITCH (1/4 X)
Quarter Stitches are denoted by triangular shapes of color in chart and color key. Come up at 1 (Fig. 5), then split fabric thread to go down at 2.

Fig. 5

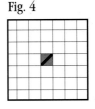

BACKSTITCH (B'ST)
For outline detail, Backstitch (shown in chart and color key by black or colored straight lines) should be worked after design has been completed (Fig. 6).

Fig. 6

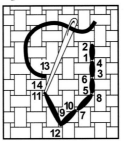

WORKING ON LINEN

Using a hoop is optional when working on linen. Roll excess fabric from left to right until stitching area is in proper position. Use sewing method when working over 2 threads. To use sewing method, keep stitching hand on right side of fabric and take needle down and up with 1 stroke. To add support to stitches, place first Cross Stitch on fabric with stitch 1-2 beginning and ending where a vertical fabric thread crosses over a horizontal fabric thread (Fig. 7).

Fig. 7

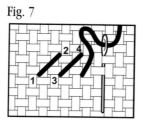

EMBROIDERY

RUNNING STITCH

Make a series of straight stitches with stitch length equal to the space between stitches (Fig. 1).

Fig. 1

STRAIGHT STITCH

Come up at 1 and go down at 2 as desired (Fig. 2).

Fig. 2

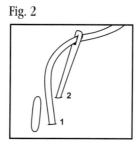

BLANKET STITCH

Referring to Fig. 3, bring needle up at 1; keeping thread below point of needle, go down at 2 and come up at 3. Continue working as shown in Fig. 4.

Fig. 3   Fig. 4

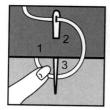 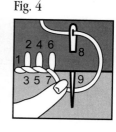

FRENCH KNOT

Bring needle up at 1 (Fig. 5); wrap floss once around needle and insert needle at 2, holding end of floss with non-stitching fingers. Tighten knot, then pull needle through fabric, holding floss until it must be released. For a larger knot, use more strands; wrap only once.

Fig. 5

CROCHET

SINGLE CROCHET

Insert hook in stitch or space indicated, YO and pull up a loop, YO and draw through both loops on hook (Fig. 1).

Fig. 1

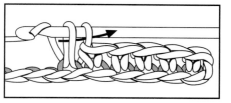

HALF DOUBLE CROCHET

YO, insert hook in stitch or space indicated, YO and pull up a loop, YO and draw through all 3 loops on hook (Fig. 2).

Fig. 2

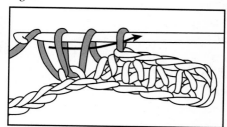

DOUBLE CROCHET

YO, insert hook in stitch or space indicated, YO and pull up a loop, YO and draw through 2 loops on hook (Fig. 3). YO and draw though remaining 2 loops on hook (Fig. 4).

Fig. 3

Fig. 4

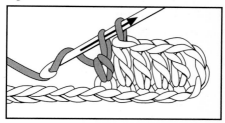

CREDITS

We want to extend a warm *thank you* to the generous people who allowed us to photograph our projects in their homes: Carl and Monte Brunck, Shirley Held, and Nancy Gunn Porter.

Sincere thanks also go to Ethan Allen Home Interiors of Little Rock, Arkansas, for allowing us to photograph our projects at their place of business.

To Magna IV Color Imaging of Little Rock, Arkansas, we say thank you for the superb color reproduction and excellent pre-press preparation.

We especially want to thank photographers Mark Mathews, Larry Pennington, Karen Shirey, and Ken West of Peerless Photography, and Jerry R. Davis of Jerry Davis Photography, all of Little Rock, Arkansas, for their time, patience, and excellent work.

To the talented people who helped in the creation of the following projects in this book, we extend a special word of thanks:

- *Silhouette Ornaments,* page 11: Polly Carbonari
- *Candy Cane Santas,* page 13: Susan Cousineau
- *Nativity Ornaments,* page 68: Linda Culp Calhoun
- *Crocheted Clothespin Angels,* page 72: Linda Luder
- *Crocheted Snowflakes,* page 73: Helen Milinkovich Milton

We extend a sincere *thank you* to the people who assisted in making and testing the projects in this book: Janice Adams, Pat Little, Judy Shirley, Diana Suttle, Karen Tyler, and Brenda Vance.